DINNER with EDWARD

Isabel Vincent

DINNER with EDWARD

A Story of an Unexpected Friendship

Pushkin Press
71–75 Shelton Street
London WC2H 9JQ

First published in the United States under the title:
Dinner with Edward: A Story of an Unexpected Friendship

Copyright © 2016 by Isabel Vincent

Published by arrangement with Algonquin Books of Chapel Hill,
a division of Workman Publishing Company, Inc., New York

First published by Pushkin Press in 2019

1 3 5 7 9 8 6 4 2

ISBN 13: 978-1-91159-026-2

All rights reserved. No part of this publication may be reproduced,
stored in a retrieval system or transmitted in any form or by any
means, electronic, mechanical, photocopying, recording or otherwise,
without prior permission in writing from Pushkin Press

Quotations on pages vii, 42, 204 and 211 from *The Gastronomical Me*
by M. F. K. Fisher, 1943 © The Estate of M. F. K. Fisher.

Offset by Tetragon, London
Printed and bound by CPI Group (UK) Ltd, Croydon, CR0 4YY

www.pushkinpress.com

For Hannah

It was one of the best meals we ever ate . . .
the fact that we remember it with such queer clarity
must mean that it had other reasons
for being important. I suppose that happens
at least once to every human. I hope so.

— M. F. K. FISHER,
The Gastronomical Me

DINNER with EDWARD

Christmas Eve Dinner

I heard about the promise Edward made to his dying wife long before I met him.

Valerie, Edward's daughter and one of my oldest friends, related the story when I saw her shortly after her mother's death. Paula, who was just shy of her ninety-fifth birthday and had been bedridden and drifting in and out of consciousness for days, sat up in bed specifically to address her beloved husband.

"Listen to me, Eddie." Paula spoke firmly, emphatically. "You can't come with me now. It would be the end of our little family."

Paula knew that Edward had already made the decision that he wanted to die rather than face life without her. That was wrong, she said, and exhorted him now to keep on living. When he finally agreed, she serenaded the man she had been married to for sixty-nine years. She began with "My Funny Valentine" and segued into half-remembered lyrics of Broadway show tunes and ballads that topped the charts in the 1940s and 1950s, when they were young and still believed that they could break into show business. Paula sang with a clear voice, unfettered by the congestion that had gurgled in her chest just days earlier and had made it impossible for her to talk. She ended with "All of You," mangling the lyrics as she went: "I love the north of you, the east, the west, and the south of you, but best of all I love all of you."

She died twenty-four hours later. It was October 2009. Overcome with grief in the days and weeks after her death, Edward found it almost impossible to keep his promise to Paula. He sat alone in a silent apartment, at the dining room table, which had been the scene of so many animated dinners. Eventually, Edward checked himself into Lenox Hill Hospital, where doctors performed a battery of tests. They couldn't find anything physically wrong with him and would be sending him home the next day.

"I'm afraid he's giving up," said Valerie, taking a seat beside me in the hospital waiting room. It was Christmas Eve and we had planned to meet for dinner. Valerie had suggested a restaurant around the corner from the hospital, where she was spending time with her father.

Settling into a table at a nondescript Third Avenue bistro, we picked at our lackluster red snapper and both of us cried. It was the day before what would have been Paula's birthday, and Valerie was still mourning her loss. Now she was also deeply worried about her father's ability to keep on living.

I'm not sure why I broke down when Valerie described Paula's serenade. I had never met Edward and, though it was a poignant scene, I can't help but think that it was also a stark reminder of my own unhappiness. I had recently moved to New York to work as a newspaper reporter and I would be spending Christmas on assignment. My marriage was unraveling, despite my best efforts to pretend that nothing was wrong. And I was more than a little concerned about the impact on my young daughter. When I hinted at my own predicament—I did not want to burden Valerie with my own problems when her father was ill—she suggested I have dinner with Edward.

"He's a great cook," Valerie said through tears, perhaps hoping that this in itself would spark my curiosity, and I would volunteer to look in on Edward after she returned to her home in Canada. Her sister Laura, an artist, lived in Greece with her husband.

I don't know if the temptation of a good meal did it for me, or if I was just so lonely that even the prospect of spending time with a depressed nonagenarian seemed appealing. It was probably a combination of loyalty to Valerie and curiosity about her father that propelled me to Edward's door a couple of months later. Whatever it was, I could never have imagined that meeting Edward would change my life.

For our very first dinner à deux, I arrived wearing a black linen shift and sandals. I knocked quietly, then rang the doorbell, and moments later a tall, elderly gentleman abruptly opened the door, his eyes smiling as he took my hand and kissed me on both cheeks.

"Darling!" he said. "I've been expecting you."

1

Grilled Sirloin Steak, Sauce Bourguignonne
New Potatoes
Chocolate Soufflé
Malbec

In the beginning I would invariably arrive at Edward's apartment with a bottle of wine.

"No need to bring anything, baby," he said, although I often ignored the advice, finding it difficult to show up for dinner empty-handed.

And there was no need to knock on the door or ring the doorbell, Edward told me. He always knew when I was coming because the doorman would call up to his apartment when I walked through the front doors of his building. Besides, he usually kept his door unlocked. Still, soon after we met he insisted that I have my own key, just in case the door *was* locked and I wanted to drop by when he was taking his morning or afternoon nap on the couch. He gave me the key attached to a purple plastic fob. EDWARD and his telephone number were written in bold, block letters on the white insert in the key ring. We both knew I would never actually use the key to get into his apartment but I accepted it graciously—a gesture of friendship, a daily reminder that Edward was now part of my life.

Whenever I did bring wine, Edward would write my name on the label, then tuck it into his makeshift cellar in the hall closet, where he kept winter coats. By the time I got there, he had already chosen his wines carefully for the meal and would save my offering for a more appropriate pairing.

At one early dinner I had made the mistake of bringing Edward some of the salted cod croquettes that I had cooked from my mother's recipe. I should never have expected him to serve them with our meal. I sprung the food on him without any warning. In those early days of our friendship I never imagined the amount of thought and effort that Edward put into each dinner. I knew it was a faux pas as soon as I handed over the lumpy tinfoil-wrapped bundle of croquettes, and I could see Edward was momentarily confused. But he graciously accepted my offering, inviting me to dinner later in the week so that we could enjoy them together.

Edward was neither a snob nor an insufferable foodie. He just liked to do things properly. He cared deeply about everything he created—whether it was the furniture in his living room or his writing. He had built and upholstered all of the furniture himself and wrote out his poems and short stories in longhand, patiently rewriting each draft on unlined white paper until he felt it was good enough to be typed by one of his daughters. He treated cooking much the same way, even though he had started doing it late in life, in his seventies. "Paula cooked for fifty-two years, and one day I just told her she'd done enough work, and now it was my turn," he said.

Edward had learned from a young age to appreciate fine food. When he was fourteen, after he failed his year at school, Edward's parents had sent him from their home in Nashville to spend a summer with his wealthy aunt and uncle in New Orleans. His aunt Eleanor, a teacher, was determined to instill discipline and get him back on track. But she was also determined to instruct him about French cuisine.

“I had an introduction to a world I didn’t know existed,” he said, recalling a meal at the legendary Antoine’s in 1934. “I will never forget the first time I had soft-shell crabs. They were fried in a light batter and served with hot melted butter. They were just delicious.”

When he started cooking, he borrowed from Antoine’s French-Creole menu, but he liked to tell me that he also appreciated the simplest things. He could still remember as a boy eating boiled cabbage, with “a gob of butter on it, which elevated it to the heavens!” And he sought inspiration everywhere: He claimed that he picked up his trick for scrambled eggs from St. John.

St. John?

He was a cook on Amtrak. “His whole life people just called him ‘Boy,’” said Edward, who met him on a ten-hour train journey he once took with Paula. “After he joined the Baptist church and was taken under the wing of a cook named Miss Emma, he started calling himself St. John the Baptist.”

St. John had a knack for eggs. When Edward asked him the secret of his scrambled eggs, St. John told him that he never cooked them all at once; he did it in a few steps. Edward had shared the trick with Paula and now insisted on showing it to me. He took farm-fresh eggs, their yolks glistening orange as he cracked them into a bowl, whisking them with a splash of milk or cream, salt, and pepper. Then he melted sweet butter in a hot frying pan, adding only half the egg mixture to the skillet when the butter was just on the edge of turning brown.

"Never all at once," Edward repeated. "You do the eggs in two steps."

After the first part began to sizzle and bubble, Edward gently loosened the eggs with a spoon, reduced the heat, and added the rest, cooking the slippery, pale yellow mixture until the eggs were light, fluffy, and completely coated in butter.

Years of childhood hardship in the South had taught Edward to be resourceful. He saved fresh herbs in Ziploc bags in the freezer, quartered the lard he bought in blocks from his Queens butcher and carefully wrapped each in waxed paper for storage in his refrigerator. Edward loved to shop at specialty food stores such as Citarella and Gourmet Garage but he happily made do at his local supermarket. He didn't own any fancy kitchen implements, and the few cookbooks I saw, which he almost never opened, had been gifts from well-meaning friends.

"It's just cooking, darling," he said, when I asked why he didn't use cookbooks. "I don't ever think of what I'm doing in terms of recipes. I just don't want to bother looking at recipes. To me, that's not cooking—being tied to a piece of paper." He hung his old but immaculately polished pots and skillets on a pressed-wood pegboard coated in tinfoil in his kitchen.

I marveled at his resourcefulness but also knew he had his own rarefied tastes. He used only Hendricks gin in a martini or when making gravlax, insisting that the cucumber essence brought out the best flavor in cured salmon. For martinis, he mixed Hendricks with dry vermouth in a Pyrex measuring cup and chilled the mixture and the glasses in the freezer until his guests arrived. Edward's martinis were neither shaken nor stirred—he simply poured gin and dry vermouth into a measuring cup and allowed the mixture to become ice-cold. He garnished each glass with a small piece of cucumber that he had also chilled until it was cold and crisp.

Whenever his elder daughter, Laura, who brought her own culinary peculiarities back from Greece when she returned to live in New York, extolled the merits of olive oil in a piecrust, Edward winced. She suspected he was giving away the golden olive oil peach pies she made for him. "When it comes to cooking or baking, he's very specific about some things," Laura said.

But the steaks Edward was grilling tonight in a hot cast-iron grill pan came from the meat fridge at the grocery store. They had been marinating in balsamic vinegar and now he seared them to perfection, laying them out on dinner plates he had warmed in the oven. The fatty juices from the steak bled across the expanse of the white porcelain, mingling with the small mound of new potatoes that he had boiled in their skins and topped with a dab of butter and chopped parsley. Then Edward swirled a velvety brown sauce on the meat before he brought the plates to the table.

The steaks were perfectly tender and tasted as though they could have come from the best butcher in Manhattan, rather than Gristedes. The sauce was buttery and rich. When I asked him how he had made it he launched into a long explanation, one that required him to take two trips to the kitchen to show me the demi-glace that was the basis for most of the sauces he made.

"Demi-glace is a long process," Edward said, pulling out a small plastic container from his refrigerator of the brown sauce that he had made from simmering roasted veal bones and vegetables until the mixture had reduced by more than three quarters and was thick and gelatinous. Like many French chefs, Edward uses demi-glace, or "glaze," as he likes to pronounce it, as a starting point for sauces and even to enrich soups.

"You can't just wish it there," he continued, referring to the long prep time. "It's not going to happen. It just cooks and cooks for days, becoming more and more concentrated."

I nodded my comprehension and spoke in hushed tones about how wonderful everything tasted. Not because I was trying to please him, but because I was truly in awe. For Edward, cooking was not just about satisfying hunger. Cooking was a passion and sometimes a serious art form, to be shared with a select few. He refused to provide tips or write out his recipes for people he felt had no affinity for cooking. As he poured some Malbec, he told me about another dinner guest who had raved about his chicken paillard.

Oh, Edward, you must give me the recipe!

But Edward told me he had no intention of sharing his paillard secrets with her. "Real cooking requires devotion," he pronounced. "And I could tell she was not devoted."

I've learned a lot about cooking from Edward. He has taught me to make the most sublime roast chicken using a paper bag and a handful of herbs, to create the perfect pastry ("Butter, and a little bit of lard in the dough, darling"), and to sprinkle balsamic vinegar on pasta to allow the sauce to cling. But from the beginning of our relationship, I knew instinctively that his culinary tips went far beyond the preparation of food. He was teaching me the art of patience, the luxury of slowing down and taking the time to think through everything I did.

When I asked him for a lesson in deboning a chicken in order to make a galantine, I knew that what Edward would end up imparting was far weightier than the butchery of poultry. In hindsight, I realize he was forcing me to deconstruct my own life, to cut it back to the bone and examine the entrails, no matter how messy that proved to be.

EDWARD LIVED ON ROOSEVELT Island in a stately co-op with wide terraces, poured concrete hallways, a sunken swimming pool, and large picture windows overlooking the East River.

I had recently moved to Roosevelt Island at my husband's insistence in a last-ditch effort to save our marriage. Unlike Edward, I was a reluctant inhabitant. A year earlier we had relocated to Manhattan from Toronto with our young daughter so that I could take up an offer to work as an investigative reporter at the *New York Post.* We had been living a few blocks from Hannah's school on the Upper East Side, and a day didn't go by that my husband didn't rail at our confined quarters, the crowds on the subways, the garbage-strewn playgrounds in our neighborhood, and alternate-side-of-the-street parking—that twice-a-week municipally ordained torture only New York City vehicle owners understand.

Maintaining a car in New York is a logistical nightmare. If you park on city streets, as do many New Yorkers who cannot afford the $400 or more monthly garage fees, you need to move your car twice a week in order to accommodate the city's street cleaners. Because parking spots are at such a premium, most drivers move their cars across the street and sit double-parked in their vehicles for the hour and a half that it takes the street sweepers to do their job. Then they quickly slide back to their old spots.

For me, alternate side parking was but a minor inconvenience, a quaint and necessary hardship of city life. It's true I wasn't the one who had to sit in the car for an hour and a half until the street-sweeping trucks passed by. But there were other nuisances, such as lugging heavy bags of groceries on the subway, exorbitant prices for just about everything in Manhattan, rushing the wrong way through the wall of rush-hour crowds to get to an assignment, or to collect Hannah from school. I felt these were small issues, endured by everyone around me—all of us part of an exclusive fraternity of the shared frustration that is life in New York City.

In fact, having spent most of my professional life reporting from the developing world, I loved the chaos of New York. The city is its own third world country, with its snarling traffic, its overflowing garbage cans, its corrupt politicians, and its rats that scurry across darkened streets and subway tracks. On muggy summer days, I kept the windows open in our apartment to welcome the clamor of the traffic and construction.

"You're crazy," said Melissa, my colleague and new friend at the *Post*. A native New Yorker, she always longed for peace and quiet.

Those first months in the city, though, I was clearly out of my depth. One day I stood waiting for the 6 train at rush hour. I was in midtown and hurrying to pick up Hannah uptown. The subway platform was crowded three deep, and the approaching train was packed. I turned to a well-dressed and frail elderly woman standing next to me.

"Wow, I really don't think we're going to get on this train," I said, surveying the crowds.

She gave me a look that I can only describe as a mixture of pity and contempt. "Where are you *from*?" she asked.

"Canada," I said, sheepishly.

"You're definitely not getting on this train," she said with a smile.

Then I watched as this refined creature clutched her buttery leather handbag, and gently but purposefully nudged herself into the crowded train. She never had to push to squeeze into the packed subway car. There was an elegance and grace in the way she inserted herself into the train just before the conductor slammed the doors shut.

I waited for the next train. It was also crowded, but in that split second as the doors burst open, I became a New Yorker. Without any fanfare, with no "excuse me" or "so sorry," I joined the crowd and slipped onto the train.

My husband refused to adapt, and a week didn't pass that I wasn't greeted with a time limit on our stay in what to him was the worst place on earth. "One more year, and that's it," he would say. But it was more than our move to New York that was threatening our marriage. We had long carried our emotional baggage over two continents. We were constantly in motion, packing and unpacking boxes, arranging furniture at the different houses we owned, filling out long government forms seeking visas to travel to places as diverse as Kosovo and Brazil. All of this prevented us from dealing with our fraying relationship. When the bitterness bubbled to the surface, when the tension increased, we craved new vistas. And so after unsuccessfully settling in a cramped apartment on the Upper East Side, we decided to try another part of the city, both of us still convinced that real estate would save our faltering marriage.

Roosevelt Island had an affordable parking garage, even though it was dilapidated, with a leaking roof and barely functioning elevator. And the nearly two-mile-long island seemed to be a pleasant retreat from the chaos of Manhattan, yet easily accessible by tram and subway to midtown. In the spring, the promenade facing Manhattan's East Side is crowded with parents pushing babies in strollers, joggers, and couples holding hands. On summer nights, the smell of grilled beef lingers in the heavy air as residents gather at the barbecue pits that line the northern end of the island. There is a riverside café, which affords spectacular views of the United Nations, and tugboats chugging back and forth under the Queensboro Bridge.

And so a few months after I ate dinner with Valerie in the Upper East Side restaurant on Christmas Eve, I found myself living just blocks from Edward. Our meals gradually became weekly events. I knew he looked forward to them as much as I did. He spent hours writing out recipes for me and giving me rather frank opinions about how I was leading my life. He was still mourning his beloved Paula and I was starting to see just how unhappy I was in my marriage.

But whatever happened in the world outside Edward's Roosevelt Island apartment, dinner was a magical interlude. We shared cocktails, a bottle of wine, and whatever

Edward was inspired to cook that day. Ella Fitzgerald, Billie Holiday, and Ute Lemper sang in the background, but sometimes there was just comfortable silence and the wind whistling outside his fourteenth floor windows.

2

Flounder, Poached in Vermouth, Sauce Fumet
Pommes de Terre Sarladaises
Baby Spinach
Avocado Salad, Homemade Blue Cheese Dressing
Apricot Soufflés
Martinis, Vouvray

I arrived at Edward's apartment just before sunset, walking the few blocks from my own apartment on the island, along the East River promenade, toward the Queensboro Bridge, negotiating little clusters of pushcarts and cyclists speeding along the riverside track. It was springtime, and the cherry trees that lined the promenade were bursting with white and pink blossoms, offering what I am sure must have been picture-postcard views of Roosevelt Island to those who lived on the other side of the river in Manhattan.

Alerted to my arrival by his doorman, Edward had already made me a martini by the time I took the elevator to the fourteenth floor. The glass was cold and the cocktail was topped with a perfect icy patina. It sat on the Formica kitchen counter next to a plastic container of goose fat, which Edward was planning to use to fry slices of parboiled potatoes. Edward had performed this trick before—peeling the skin off the small and slightly shriveled spuds, slicing them as thinly as possible and turning them into pommes de terres Sarladaises, a dish named after a medieval town—Sarlat—in the Dordogne region of France. The area was famous for its goose fat. Sometimes, just after panfrying the potato slices to a crispy, yet silky, perfection, he would toss in fresh parsley and minced garlic.

Edward had already warmed two dinner plates and piled each with a mound of baby spinach. He was poaching flounder in vermouth. When the fish was ready, he would spoon it on top of the spinach and add the sauce fumet, which he made from sautéed fish bones, white wine, carrots, onions, and butter. The sauce wilted the spinach until it was just slightly undercooked.

As usual, he refused my offers to help him prepare dinner. "Stay out there!" he ordered, pointing to the living room. I sat in an easy chair sipping my martini and looking out as dusk began to fall and lights twinkled from the buildings that stood against the river on the Manhattan side. Ella Fitzgerald crooned in the background, "There's a somebody I'm longing to see, I hope that he turns out to be someone to watch over me . . ."

It was clearly a female presence who watched over us in Edward's apartment. Months after her death, Paula was still here. Edward had taped several color photocopies of her last photograph to the walls of the living and dining rooms. Although her face was lined with wrinkles, I would be hard pressed to describe her as elderly, even though she was well into her nineties when the photo was taken. She was resplendent in red lipstick and dangly earrings, her chin slightly raised in an air of self-assuredness, defiance even. Edward placed the photos at different angles so that he could talk to Paula when he cooked, look up at her when he made dinner or sat on the sofa to read a book.

After she died, Edward began writing her letters, telling her about what he had cooked that day, which of their friends he had bumped into. Shortly after we met, he started to write to Paula about me. "Paula would have liked you because you have fabric—character," he said to me.

Despite the little I knew about either Edward or Paula at that point, I was both flattered and reassured that Edward and I were becoming friends. Now the minutiae of my life—my adventures in the city working for the *Post*, my crumbling marriage, the difficulties of raising my daughter—filled Edward's thoughts and his letters to Paula. Soon he became so wrapped up in helping me navigate my middle age that sorting out my problems dispelled the dark notions that had weighed on him after Paula died.

Not that I confided much in those early days, beyond the indignities of my new job working at a tabloid in the world's most competitive media center.

"The editors yell at reporters in the newsroom!" I told Edward, reminding him that I had cut my teeth as a reporter at a Canadian newspaper, a far more genteel place than the *Post*'s aggressive newsroom, where one of the first communications I received from my editor was an e-mail with "WTF?" in the subject header.

That same week, my boss, a stocky, tough-talking Puerto Rican–Irish newsman, completely deleted a story

I wrote about an environmental charity run by the musician Sting and insisted I rewrite it on the spot. I am sure most veteran reporters would have been offended but I took it in stride, even though I had more than twenty years' experience in journalism, much of it spent as a foreign correspondent.

In New York, though, I was always reporting by the seat of my pants. An Australian intern I met put it best: "It's news on steroids." Still, I was astounded when, after reading the Sting piece, my editor took a gulp of his impossibly beige half and half–infused coffee and pressed the delete button.

"This is how you write a story," he barked, pointing a stubby finger at the now blank computer screen. "Statement! Quote to back it up! Statement! Quote to back it up . . ."

Despite the harshness of the newsroom, where my rickety computer always seemed to freeze in the minutes before deadline and the printers broke down several times a day, I was also making good friends. My best friend became the woman who sat in the cubicle next to the one I was assigned during my first week at work. As I told Edward, Melissa and I were polar opposites. Where she was impeccably coiffed and elegantly dressed, with perfectly lacquered fingernails and precise bangs, I was disheveled, usually arriving late for work after dropping off Hannah at school, my nails chipped, my hair windblown. She once gave me a hairbrush as a gift.

I called Melissa when I got lost in the city, which was often. Another friend referred to her as my personal GPS. She even knew where to stand in any given subway station to be closest to the exit you wanted when the train arrived at your stop. She had an app on her phone for that. When I went on assignment alone, she made sure I was armed with a paper map because I had trouble deciphering directions on my phone.

We became fast friends, our connection forged in what she called "the paragraph factory" and what I more sinisterly dubbed "the gulag" of tabloid journalism. "It's like breaking rocks at the gulag," I said, every time our copy came back with a long list of questions, the answers to which we were asked to provide in the minutes before deadline, and we knew they would never make it into the paper. Our editors thought nothing of sending us out on an assignment at four a.m. to attend Friday prayers at a mosque in lower Manhattan or stake out the alleged mistress of a senator in suburban New Jersey, sitting for hours in a hot car in high summer.

"What's wrong with you?" barked my editor into the phone when I lost sight of the senator's mistress because I left my post for a half hour to buy water and go to the bathroom. While I was gone, she had gotten into her car and left home. My trail went cold.

"YOU CAN'T GO TO THE BATHROOM DURING A STAKEOUT!" my editor screamed in what seemed to me all caps. "You go to the bathroom before a stakeout or after a stakeout but NEVER DURING A STAKEOUT!"

I regaled Edward with tales of the *Post* newsroom, emphasizing the humor and the characters I was meeting, but though my stories often made him laugh, they also gave him pause. Edward thought I was working too hard, that I needed to ask myself some serious questions about what I really wanted to achieve.

"You know," said Edward, after I told him about an episode at work, "I've never really seen you laugh, in a loud voice, with your head tossed back, like you are really enjoying it." Edward refilled my glass with the crisp

Vouvray we were drinking and we both started on our avocado salads, using thinly sliced pieces of baguette to lap up Edward's pungent blue cheese dressing.

A few days later a letter arrived in the mail, in Edward's familiar script, on cream-colored stationery attached to a photocopy of the recipe that had inspired his apricot soufflé I had complimented at dinner. He had clipped it from the *New York Times* in the early 1990s when he first started cooking for Paula and their friends and family. Despite his prejudice against following recipes, he had obviously kept a few favorites over the years. It was labor-intensive, calling for dried apricots that had to be boiled and pureed, then chilled for several hours before they could be added to the stiffened egg whites.

Edward had made us individual soufflés in little ramekins, putting them in the oven as we began our main course. He served them immediately after they were done, their puffy meringue swirls tinged golden brown and looking like the whimsical domes of some dreamy cathedral from a fairy tale, dusted with confectioners' sugar and topped with freshly whipped cream. There was magic in Edward's fluffy confection. That first time—and every time after that he made it for me—I savored each spoonful as the swirl of cream, meringue, and apricot melted in my mouth.

Though our early dinners were not gloomy, it's likely that Edward had already picked up on my matrimonial woes. Appropriately, in the letter that accompanied the soufflé recipe, Edward felt compelled to warn me against living an unromantic life: "That is a somber thought," he wrote. "For as I have tried to remind you, there is much about you that is not just attractive but very lovable. As important as career is to women, they must not forget who they are and what they are."

Edward came of age in the 1950s when a good career choice for a woman was being a housewife. After all, Paula gave up her dream of becoming an actress and stayed at home to raise their two daughters. Edward took a series of jobs to keep the family afloat. But they were no ordinary suburban couple. In their spare time they wrote plays; Paula even wrote a young adult novel, which she managed to have published. Edward's advice to me was clearly drawn from his personal experience and was at times tinged with sexism. But, strangely, I didn't really notice, not until other women pointed it out to me. I saw Edward through such a benevolent lens that it never occurred to me to question his wisdom. For on some level I felt he was correct—I was working so hard that I had neglected many things about myself. And listening to him talk about Paula, I was beginning to see just how doomed my own marriage was.

"I'm a man who loves women, for all the obscure reasons as well as the obvious ones," Edward wrote to me in a letter shortly after we met. "Their femininity, their charm, desirability, delicacy, warmth, beauty, tenderness and on and on—a list too long to record. But I have only been in love with one woman all my mature life."

To say Edward loved his wife is an understatement. "I wouldn't have lived this long without her," he would tell me repeatedly about the woman he first saw in New York in the waning days of summer in 1940.

In the thick scrapbooks and photo albums he keeps on the shelves of his living room, Edward seems to have every letter he exchanged with his wife, every theater program, restaurant business card, and handmade Thanksgiving dinner menu adorned with pressed autumn leaves.

The first volume, which dates back to the year he met Paula, begins with the unembellished black-and-white photos that they took of each other on a beach in California ("We always took interesting pictures, never normal," he told me). The photos of Edward and Paula—both tall, lanky, young—are accompanied by descriptions on index cards, cut to fit the photo album pages and written in Edward's loping hand.

Then there are the pages and pages of plastic-covered birthday and Valentine cards. On Paula's eighty-fifth birthday, Edward wrote, "How I ever got you is beyond belief. So don't wake me up at this date—just let me go on thinking that I'm special enough to deserve you!" In a card to her husband, written at about the same time, Paula wrote, "To my own Eddie: We dreamed we'd get to the top of the mountain, and here we are. I'll be lovin' you, always!"

Tonight, flipping through the cards and letters between Edward and Paula, I casually mentioned that I had never sent anyone a Valentine's Day card (not since grade school, anyway). Sadly, I had never thought to send one to my husband, even in the early days of our relationship when I still lived in an illusion of happiness. And since moving to New York we had grown so far apart that there seemed no breaching the chasm.

Edward was silent, as if suddenly suspended in a state of disbelief. He leaned over the table, poured us the remaining drops of the Vouvray, and then we both lingered over the last spoonfuls of our apricot soufflés.

A few days later, when Edward's recipe came in the mail—along with his admonition to be more romantic—I set out to make the soufflés on my own. I removed the eggs from the refrigerator, making sure they were at room temperature, heated the apricots with sugar, and allowed them to chill in the refrigerator before mixing in the rest of the ingredients.

"This recipe never fails," Edward had told me. And he was right, because for one of my first renditions I used fresh apricots and my soufflé turned out bland. The puréed dried apricots, which were packed with flavor, made for a richer, more complex dessert.

I would eventually learn to follow Edward's recipes with a heightened degree of precision, whether they were instructions for the preparation of food or for life. His assertions never veered too far from certain fundamental themes—he spoke about recognizing "the stranger in all of us" and achieving what he liked to call "a resting place of the soul," by which I now realize he meant self-assurance and being happy in your own skin. Or as he put it, "a place in your head where you are at peace with your life, with your decisions."

3

Scrod, in San Marzano Tomato Sauce
Orange Zest Salad
Apple Galette, Vanilla Ice Cream
Pinot Grigio

In the nineteenth century Roosevelt Island, then known as Blackwell's Island, was crowded with more than a dozen prisons, a smallpox hospital, workhouses, and even a home for "wayward girls." Municipal leaders in the growing metropolis across the river decided that Blackwell's Island would be the perfect place to lock away the criminal, the indigent, and the insane, convinced that "the pleasant and glad surroundings would be conducive to both physical and mental rehabilitation." In 1828, New York City purchased the island for $32,000 and, four years later, the Blackwell's Island penitentiary and hospital opened.

When I moved to the island in 2010, nearly fourteen thousand people—many of them UN bureaucrats and émigrés from the former Yugoslavia—lived among the remnants of that sad history. There are still the ghostly skeletons of abandoned hospitals, and even the modern residential buildings, most of them completed in the 1970s, resemble correctional facilities, minus bars and barbed wire fencing. Inside, the stained carpets in the hallways smell of cigarette smoke and stale cabbage. By contrast, Edward's building is one of the more elegant and well maintained, with a small army of solicitous doormen.

During the year I lived on Roosevelt Island, there were few restaurants and only a Starbucks and a supermarket that residents referred to as the "antique store" because many of the products were past their "best before" dates. The island, which is about eight hundred feet wide at its widest point, turns into a ghost town after dark. When I invited an eighty-year-old friend who had lived in Manhattan for most of her life to visit me, she looked suspiciously around a deserted Main Street at night, and tentatively asked where she might find the wine store.

"Astoria," I said.

Returning to Manhattan on the tram, a fellow rider mistook her for a tourist and asked where she was from.

"Manhattan," she deadpanned.

We had rented an apartment in a sprawling housing complex right past the Good Shepherd Church and the Roosevelt Island Garden Club, with its odd, labyrinthine plots, crowded in summer with a lush tangle of tomato vines, all manner of flowering shrubs, and a jumble of dusty lawn ornaments.

But where my husband at least at first saw paradise, I began to focus on something entirely different, and I started to pine for the bustling, vibrant streets of Manhattan. There was something about Roosevelt Island that seemed to mirror my own sadness. A legless beggar on a hospital gurney regularly greeted commuters with a tin can when they emerged from the subway station. I was soon to discover that he was part of the community of amputees who were residents of the two rehabilitation hospitals that were somber reminders of the island's grim past.

We lived in The Octagon, the site of the former New York City Lunatic Asylum. The apartments were massive, with stunning views of the Manhattan skyline.

The building had a tennis court, an outdoor pool, an art gallery, and even a little shuttle bus that ferried residents to the subway and tram stations. In 2006, a Manhattan developer had transformed The Octagon into a luxury rental building, unusual for the island, complete with marble countertops, high ceilings, and designer fixtures in "the dramatic setting of an urban waterfront park."

But the brochures said nothing about 888 Main Street's dark history as one of the most notorious institutions in nineteenth-century New York—a place that even Charles Dickens found too creepy to spend much time at. "Everything had a lounging, listless, madhouse air, which was very painful," Dickens writes in *American Notes for General Circulation*, after a truncated tour in 1842. "The moping idiot, cowering down with long dishevelled hair; the gibbering maniac, with his hideous laugh and pointed finger; the vacant eye, the fierce wild face, the gloomy picking of the hands and lips, and munching of the nails: there they were all, without disguise, in naked ugliness and horror."

More than forty years later, the *New York Times* reported on thirty-five-year-old Ellen Drum, a patient who suffered from "melancholia" and had been at the lunatic asylum for nearly two years. She had left the asylum dressed in "only a calico dress and undergarments and stockings" and was presumed drowned in the river. Her body was never found. There was something chilling about the eerie silences that descended on The Octagon at night. In retrospect, it was probably the most appropriate place in New York City for a breakdown, which I was soon to have. "I feel a deep emptiness—like nothing I have ever known," I wrote in my journal, shortly after arriving at the island. "I have to do something drastic to end this."

The sadness stemmed from loneliness. Despite our moving to Roosevelt Island at his request, my husband still hated New York so much that every school holiday and summer vacation became excuses to leave town with Hannah. Sometimes he didn't even need the excuse and left on his own. When his mother became ill in Canada, I tried to be sympathetic but he was gone for increasingly long periods. We had spent most of our savings moving to New York; my husband didn't have a green card, so I had no choice but to work to support all of us. In the mornings, I took the subway to my midtown office, and came home late at night to a cold, too-big apartment, overlooking the lights of Manhattan.

I began to count on dinner with Edward as a much-needed respite. His apartment became a sanctuary. One day, as I walked off the elevator on Edward's floor, I immediately inhaled cinnamon, sugar, and baked apples and I felt a rush of happiness. Edward had made his famous apple galette. I zeroed in on it as soon as I walked into his kitchen, where it sat cooling on a piece of oven-browned parchment.

Before meeting Edward, I had baked apple pies only with Crisco crusts or strudels made with sheets of frozen filo dough that were too fussy to work with. His galette was wonderfully rustic—a hearty-looking apple tart, the pastry roughly folded over at the sides like an envelope, the buttery apple slices flecked with cinnamon and oozing caramelized fruit, generously dusted with confectioners' sugar.

Edward topped it with a dollop of cream or vanilla ice cream, so that the tartness of the apple was bathed in a melting sweet, white puddle on the plate. It was so good that I could barely remember what else we had for dinner on the night I first tried it. I believe it was some kind of fish, maybe scrod in a delicate sauce of plump San Marzano tomatoes—the only kind he ever used—and a salad with long pieces of orange zest in a light vinaigrette. Whatever we ate clearly paled in my memory.

"You need to send me the recipe!" I said.

Edward demurred and poured me the rest of the pinot grigio. He went to the refrigerator to retrieve another bottle of wine and when he returned he said he would try to put something together for me. He had never written it down, he said. But a few days after that first bite, I received handwritten instructions on a white piece of paper, labeled simply "Pastry." It included the following directions:

3 ice cubes—crushed in heavy plastic bag with mallet
2 tbs frozen lard (optional but excellent addition)

There were copious notes about the importance of keeping the butter, the lard, and even the mixing bowl as cold as possible. It was imperative that I put everything—the mixing bowl, the flour, and any baking tools I was planning to use—in the freezer before proceeding with the recipe. He also insisted that I use a cheese grater to grate a frozen stick of butter into the flour mixture.

I could deal with the grated butter and the frozen

bowl, but later, when I tried to duplicate Edward's pastry, I would find it almost impossible to work the crushed ice into the pastry dough. The ice simply wouldn't hold the flour and butter together. Maybe it needed to be turned into slush? After several attempts, I despaired. I didn't own a food processor ("How can you live without one, darling?" asked Edward), so I used my hands. Half the dough seemed to stick to my fingers, and the rest was too stiff and powdery to work with. Why couldn't he just use ice water? It was good enough for Julia Child, after all.

But Edward was adamant that the secret to the perfect galette pastry was crushed ice. And, of course, the apples. Edward preferred a Cortland or a Macoun over a Macintosh for a galette. The Cortland had a firmer texture, he said, so it wouldn't dissolve into mush when you sautéed it in butter, lemon juice, and sugar and then baked it in a hot oven. The Macintosh was too porous, absorbed too much water, and usually fell apart, he said.

Indeed, the apples in Edward's galettes were always firm and tart with just the right hint of sweetness. He bought the apples at the Mennonite farmers' market under the Roosevelt Island Bridge underpass on Saturday mornings, and always baked galettes for Thanksgiving dinner, which he still celebrated with his friends who lived just up Main Street.

The truth is I didn't tackle Edward's galette until much, much later. At this time I was so lonely that I often didn't feel like cooking, especially when my husband and daughter were away. Cooking for myself in our huge kitchen, with its showroom stainless steel appliances and cold, sleek countertops, seemed daunting. My worn pots looked threadbare against this backdrop of sterile opulence, so I rarely ate anything I had to spend any time preparing. And because I stopped going grocery shopping when my family was away, there was often no food in the refrigerator anyway. On Friday nights, after working late, I often sat in front of the TV watching a documentary on, say, the Holocaust and eating from a can of sardines.

"Oh, will you stop with the pity party," Melissa often said, when I described to her my typical Friday evening. But it wasn't exactly a pity party. The sardines were always the best I could find—in olive oil, wild-caught from the cold waters off the coast of Galicia in Spain. Melissa encouraged me to order in or go out to eat. But going out for dinner by myself seemed unlikely. Shortly after moving to Manhattan, my husband and I had passed a smartly dressed young woman in a restaurant, sitting at a table set for one, reading a book and sipping a glass of white wine.

"That's the problem with women here; they're all lonely," said my husband. "I don't want my daughter turning into that."

But although I nodded my agreement, I secretly admired the diner's cozy solitude—she was sitting, reading, savoring the wine and her own company. Years later, I read the extraordinary food writer M. F. K. Fisher's own experiences of dining as a single woman in the late 1930s and early 1940s.

"More often than not people who see me on trains and in ships, or in restaurants, feel a kind of resentment of me since I taught myself to enjoy being alone," she wrote in 1938. After the death of her husband, Fisher confessed to her readers that "sometimes I would go to the best restaurant I knew about, and order dishes and good wines as if I were a guest of myself, to be treated with infinite courtesy."

I longed to be a guest of myself, but I was far from articulating that desire and I had not yet discovered M. F. K.

Fisher, or Julia Child for that matter. When I finally read Fisher's essays about her life and food in *The Gastronomical Me*, I came to understand that sense of peace that eluded me and that I had so admired in the Manhattan tableau of the woman at the restaurant table set for one. This was surely part of what Edward was talking about when he spoke about the "resting place of the soul."

I, on the other hand, still suffered from an agonized soul, and on Roosevelt Island, the ghosts of the asylum haunted me. I was not at peace, and the specter of disrupting my daughter or spending the rest of my life alone stifled my will to fight. I set about trying to placate everyone around me, pondering how to make others happy. I realize now it was wrongheaded and simply added to my own misery. On the day after my birthday—February 5, 2011—all I wrote in my journal was, "In a real dark night of the soul, it is always three in the morning, day after day." It was F. Scott Fitzgerald's line about depression, and I felt it keenly.

At night, I lay awake ruminating. How could I fix life in New York for my unhappy spouse so that he would spend more time in the city with me? Perhaps we could move somewhere else, to a house in Queens with a garage? Long Island? What about marriage counseling? Didn't we owe it to our daughter to try to make this work? But what could I do about the other things he complained about—the car horns, the people who walked too fast, the rush-hour subway crowds?

I knew that it wasn't so much New York that he hated. New York was just an excuse, an external manifestation of his chronic restlessness. In our nine years together, we had moved from an apartment in Toronto, to a house in Miami, back to Toronto and a grand Victorian house that we renovated. But as soon as that renovation project was completed, he sought out another one, and we moved again, and then again. After the third renovation, we were off again, this time to Rio de Janeiro, where we spent three years, the longest we had ever spent in one place. I worked on a book project in Rio, and he took mournful black-and-white pictures of Carnival. I suspect the stark images of these pre-Lenten revelers in their feathers and glitter and disguises were metaphors for his own sense of displacement.

Once we were installed on Roosevelt Island, he began to complain that I worked too much, that I wasn't home to cook, I didn't clean up properly. He even presented me with a time sheet showing me how many hours he had spent looking after our daughter, the implication being that I was not doing my fair share. His complaints grew increasingly shrill, which is when I knew that it was me that he was trying to escape during all the years we had been together. And I began to plot my own departure.

But sleep-deprived and on edge, I felt there was nowhere to go. I began to imagine that I was incarcerated, and then one morning right before dawn I glanced outside at the maze-like inner courtyard of The Octagon and I panicked. I threw jeans and a sweatshirt over my pajamas and walked to the deserted lighthouse overlooking the churning waters known as Hell Gate, a treacherous spot for boats and the scene of epic wrecks.

I sat facing the looming towers of Harlem and the Bronx, knowing I was emotionally marooned on this sliver of land surrounded on all sides by dark water.

4

Herb-Roasted Chicken in a Paper Bag
Roasted Vegetables
Fennel Rémoulade over Lettuce
Popover Flambé
Martinis, Pinot Blanc

I arrived at Edward's apartment just as the first of the winter's nor'easters was beginning to rage. I had walked the few blocks from my own apartment, along the East River promenade, toward the Queensboro Bridge, its majesty little diminished, even as it was pelted by the storm—fierce exclamation marks of snow.

When I took a seat in Edward's living room, snow obscured my view of the buildings lining the river on the Upper East Side as Manhattan seemed to grow silent, its twinkling lights barely reflected on the choppy waters. Wrapped up in the storm, I was startled when Edward suddenly called from the kitchen.

"We need to work on your feminine enhancement."

I was too shocked to say much of anything and, instead, took it as my signal to come to the table. Sitting down, I snuck a taste of fennel rémoulade, which was already dished out onto small salad plates. It was meant as a second course, but I was impatient. Edward made his rémoulade in the Louisiana style, with cayenne pepper and mayonnaise, whipping it until the mixture turned a light rose. The creamy, piquant rémoulade enveloped the slightly sweet, firm pieces of steamed fennel. I found it hard to stop eating. Luckily, Edward arrived, clutching a platter of bronzed chicken on a bed of roasted carrots and celery topped with fresh sprigs of thyme and rosemary. He had brined the chicken for two days in apple cider and salt, before rubbing the entire bird with thyme, rosemary, and butter. He chopped carrots, onions, and celery for a mirepoix, which he spooned onto parchment, and set the chicken on top. Then he wrapped everything in a paper bag and braised the chicken in the oven for hours.

Edward set down the platter on the table, steadied

himself, and took his seat. He poured wine for both of us and brandished his carving knife and fork with a slight flourish. He carefully cut into the succulent white flesh, hoisting a slice of breast meat onto my plate. When he had broken off a leg for himself, he buttered a piece of baguette and winked at me.

"Bon appétit," he said with an exaggerated French accent.

After tasting Edward's paper-bag chicken, I never roasted chicken any other way again. The paper bag never burned in a hot oven, and the chicken never dried out. Just before removing it from the oven, he ratcheted up the heat to 500 degrees and removed the bag so that the skin was slightly charred and crispy.

"This is fantastic," I told him after my first bite, crunching through the skin to the tender meat.

Edward happily agreed, but he had other things on his mind and now returned to his views on my femininity.

I knew that he didn't mean to be unkind; Edward felt he was simply stating facts. He said it with the authority of age, with the certainty that he didn't have time to waste, and since he was imparting to me the ultimate truth, he didn't need to mince words. The thought that he might hurt my feelings never crossed his mind. By now I was used to these life lessons from Edward that were direct and with no preamble. He told me I needed to set a strong example for Hannah, and that he sensed that I was "in a ditch, going in circles" in my marriage.

At a previous dinner, when for the first time I really told him some of the details of my faltering marriage, and how I was too afraid to take any definitive steps for fear of traumatizing my young daughter, Edward was silent. A few days later, I received a letter that I still take out to read when I am feeling besieged. He noted, in part, "You are a fine and talented woman, whose potential is yet to be realized given the love and support and luck we all need. Where you lost the will to fight for what is yours, where you gave away control of your life, is the mystery you are now unraveling. When you get it all back, hold on to it."

At ninety-three, Edward is almost twice my age. Born in Nashville, he likes his bourbon on the rocks, uses words like "moxie" in conversation, but he can also curse like a New Yorker. He doesn't own a cell phone or a computer; he writes in longhand, and he never watches television.

"We live in the age of communications but nobody

knows how to communicate anymore," he once said to me. "It's just e-mailing and texting, not communicating," Edward went on. "Nobody's dealing with reality. It's a shame."

Edward occasionally reads the *New York Times* at the Roosevelt Island branch of the New York Public Library across the street from his apartment building. And whenever I have a story in the *Post,* he heads out to the deli on Main Street next to his building to buy the newspaper. He has a subscription to the *New York Review of Books* that he received as a Christmas present. He includes a photocopy of the *Times* review tucked into the inside flap of any book he reads. If it was given as a gift, he insists upon an inscription on the title page from the person who presented him with the book. He has no formal degree beyond high school, but he is one of the most educated people I know. His letters are on embossed stationery, and he sends me his handwritten poetry that sometimes makes me cry.

And he always tells me the truth, sometimes in the gentlest ways, but as I have said he can also be harsh. In many ways, he has forced me to confront traits about myself that I would much rather have remained suppressed.

Edward's insights into my own life often gave me pause, but it was his generosity that moved me to tears. I knew a great deal of thought must have preceded his comments on my appearance, but I was not prepared for what he said next.

"We need to get you something special," said Edward, as we ate. "I'd like to see you in a nice dress, some heels. We need to go shopping."

By way of explanation, he launched into a story about how he had once bought an expensive suit for his daughter Laura when he felt that she was feeling down. He had taken her to Saks Fifth Avenue, where the suit Laura chose had been reduced from $1,400 but was still costly.

"Can we afford it?" Paula asked him at the time.

"We can't afford not to," Edward replied simply. He also bought Laura an expensive trench coat.

"She looked smashing," he recalled.

Just then an alarm went off in the kitchen—the timer for the popover that Edward was baking in the oven. He stood up, a little wobbly. I rose to help him remove our plates, but he was having none of it. I knew better than to insist.

I came to understand that dinners with Edward were

rituals, imbued with a sense of occasion. When he was feeling well, Edward created feasts of cassoulet or oysters Rockefeller, and sometimes we indulged in a good champagne or port, served in the delicate one-hundred-year-old glasses he inherited from his mother. He always warmed his dinner plates in the oven, even if he was serving only leftovers—although Edward rarely served leftovers. Everything unfolded with the same comforting ceremony: There was always a cocktail before the main course—tonight we'd had martinis—followed by dessert and perhaps Turkish coffee spiked with brandy or Ricard to finish.

"The secret is treating family like guests and guests like family," he once told me. No matter how terrible I felt in the moments before I knocked on his door, I always left Edward's apartment with a smile on my face, a sensation that I had just experienced some kind of pure joy.

"I just had dinner with your father!" I told Valerie, calling her in Canada on my walk home after one of those early dinners with Edward. "Thank you! Thank you! I don't know why, but I feel great!"

Now Edward deposited our dishes in the sink, then busied himself with dessert. He poured apricot jam and cognac into a skillet and lit the mixture, stepping back slightly while flames shot out from the frying pan. When the fire died down, he spooned the flambéed apricot onto the warm popover that he had removed from the oven. Then he dusted everything with confectioners' sugar.

Maybe it was the sweet, spongy popover or the amount of wine we had consumed that evening. It was not unusual for us to split an entire bottle during a meal together. Whatever it was, I heard myself happily acquiescing to the shopping trip, and then toasting our expedition with the last of our wine.

Yes, I was now Edward's special project. I had no doubt that fixing my confused middle-aged existence was giving him some kind of purpose in life. Whatever was going on, I had already given in. But I did make him promise one thing: He would not actually *buy* me anything.

"OK," he said, his blue-gray eyes twinkling. "We'll just look."

5

Chicken Paillard, Sauce aux Champignons
Pommes de Terres Soufflés
Baked Acorn Squash
Almond Cake, Vanilla Ice Cream
Bourbon/Pastis Cocktail, Chardonnay

I watched Edward pour a finger of bourbon into a tumbler he had just removed from the freezer. He added tonic and a splash of pastis, which turned the mixture slightly cloudy. He finished the cocktail off with a squeeze of lime and added a few ice cubes from an old Tupperware container that he uses to store ice in his freezer.

It was never my favorite cocktail; I preferred his perfect martinis, ice-cold, dry and crisp. The drink Edward fashioned for me was a little too sweet for my liking, but

I never dreamed of refusing it. Sometimes, when it was available in New York liquor stores, he would substitute absinthe for the bourbon and triumphantly pour me what he liked to call the "green fairy"—aromatic with hints of fennel and anise.

Over time, I grew to enjoy Edward's concoctions; they became a necessary elixir, like the pink penicillin that my mother forced on me as a bronchitis-plagued child. And I drank it in with the advice that Edward doled out during dinner, which often stretched over three or even four courses.

"The problem with too many women is their lack of self-worth," he said. "What impressed me about Paula was her sense of self-worth." She wasn't about to be pushed around. I needed to learn to be tough, he told me. And I should try to impart that to my daughter, too.

"Did the dress arrive?" he asked as I stood in the kitchen sipping my cocktail and watching as he took frozen chunks of potatoes that he had packed into Ziploc bags and dropped them into hot grape seed oil. He had a peculiar way of making french fries that required the potatoes to be parboiled and then frozen before frying. He used only grape seed oil because it was the only oil you could heat to very high temperatures without risk of smoking or burning. The french fries, or *pommes soufflés*, comprised one of his more complicated culinary tricks that I have yet to master.

Edward sang along to Ella Fitzgerald and seemed not to care at all that he was completely out of tune: "I've got a crush on you, sweetie pie . . ."

Before I could give him an answer on the dress, Edward insisted we sit down and try the french fries while they were still hot, crisp, and perfect. Any delays might result in soggy potatoes, he warned, with such conviction that I dared not argue. As usual, he was right. What a french fry! A slab of soft potato spilling out of a crispy, golden, salty coating. Not surprisingly, the entire meal was sublime—the mushy sweetness of the squash, its pale orange flesh streaked with butter and brown sugar; the delicate paillard covered in a rich mushroom sauce, made from Edward's demi-glace, wine, and firm, buttery mushrooms.

"The dress hasn't arrived yet," I said, spearing another french fry.

Edward stopped eating, a look of concern clouding his face. I assured him that I wasn't worried, but he told me to make sure that I alerted my doorman that I was expecting a package from Saks. I promised him I would, but promptly forgot, and the dress languished in my building's package room for days before I thought to check.

After I reassured Edward about the dress, we moved on to dessert: vanilla ice cream and Edward's almond cake. It was the one he had seen in the vitrine of Payard, when it was still located in its elegant quarters on Lexington Avenue. On a whim, he duplicated the cake perfectly in his kitchen. Edward claimed he never actually tasted the Payard cake; it was enough for him to study the golden, spongy confection.

He made the same cake for my birthday, surprising me at my midtown office. A tall, courtly figure in a black quilted jacket, pressed black corduroys, and a jaunty beret, he charmed the normally humorless woman at front-desk security, who called me down with the breathless, "Edward's here with a surprise for you!"

Edward had a similar effect on the sales associates at Saks Fifth Avenue, where we had gone shopping the previous week. He insisted it had to be Saks. At the last minute, I had suggested Bloomingdale's because I wanted to save him the walk. Edward moved with difficulty, with a cane. On days when he was in pain, he walked around his small kitchen by gripping the counters with both hands, like a slow-motion gymnast on parallel bars. I didn't want him to suffer on the shopping trip and figured that because Bloomingdale's was around the corner from the Roosevelt Island tram on the Manhattan side, he might prefer to go there instead. But, no, Edward insisted on Saks and seemed not to care that it would be a longer journey, first on the local Roosevelt Island bus to the tram station, and then on another bus to Fifth Avenue.

We met at the bus stop in front of Edward's building on a bone-chillingly cold afternoon in deep winter. He immediately admonished me for not having put on enough lipstick. I rummaged in my bag for the new Dior lipstick I had bought a few days before with Melissa. Squinting at my reflection in the bus shelter, I tentatively began to reapply Rouge Favori.

When I looked sideways at Edward, he laughed, shaking his head in mock disapproval. He was clearly enjoying his role as a stern Henry Higgins to my recalcitrant Eliza Doolittle. "Put more on!" he said, tapping the cold ground with his cane for emphasis. "You're not using enough!"

Gliding over the East River on the crowded tram, Roosevelt Island disappearing behind us, Edward pointed out all the snow-covered bridges as they came into view: the Brooklyn, Williamsburg, and Manhattan Bridges to the south, the Queensboro Bridge directly beside us. As we sped closer to Manhattan, residential buildings towered on both sides of us.

We descended into the chaos of Second Avenue and waited at the bus stop on East Sixtieth. Impatient, I raised a gloved hand to hail a taxi.

"Are you in a hurry?" asked Edward in his matter-of-fact, cheerful tone, which always made me feel foolish.

When we reached our stop, I offered Edward my arm and he shifted his cane to his other hand. We locked arms and walked slowly along Fifth Avenue as snowflakes began to fall. When we reached Saks, Edward knew exactly where to go. He headed up the elevator to the second floor, with its luxurious displays of designer clothes.

A chic sales associate from the Etro boutique gave us the once-over—Edward looking like a French country gentleman with his usual old world air, a cashmere scarf neatly folded around his neck; me, somewhat ill at ease, in my scuffed Italian leather boots, faded jeans, and too-red lips. When Edward explained our mission, the Etro lady insisted on helping me select several dresses to try on. Meanwhile, Edward studied the sale racks and came back with a single dress—an elegant black, hip-hugging number with short sleeves, discreetly embellished with a piece of black lace at the waist. It was by Burberry and cost a small fortune, but Edward had looked at neither the price tag nor the label when he lifted it up to show me.

"I'd like to see how this looks on you, darling," he said, handing me the dress before taking his place in an easy chair outside the fitting rooms.

Somehow it didn't really surprise me that of all the dresses I tried on that afternoon, Edward's choice was the perfect one, even if it was a little tight. He had worked as a tailor at one point in his life, and he understood a good cut, excellent craftsmanship. Resting his chin on the handle of his cane, in deep concentration, Edward asked me to turn around before making his final pronouncement.

"It really shows off your figure," he said. "I didn't even know you had a figure. Not a great figure, but a nice figure." And then, pointing his cane in my direction, he ordered: "Stick your stomach in! Stand up straight!"

I breathed in, stood up straight, but the dress was too tight, especially around my hips, and I could barely do up the zipper in the back. Edward was right about one thing, though—for the first time in a long time I noticed that I did indeed have hips. And legs. And breasts. I was a woman, and as tight as this dress was, it also flattered me in a way that I had ignored for many years. Suddenly, I *needed* this black dress, even though I had a closet full of black dresses, most of them loose-fitting and shapeless. Edward had selected it, after all, and under the harsh lights of the fitting room I imagined that it would be a talisman, enticement, and armor all wrapped into one. I didn't even blink at the $525 price tag. It was on sale, after all, and worth every penny.

After checking her computer, the Etro lady found the dress in my size at another store. She assured me that it would arrive at my apartment in less than a week. I handed her a credit card, and our little excursion came to an end. Edward steadied himself with his cane, and rose slowly from the chair outside the fitting room as a gaggle of fashionable sales associates who had been watching us with broad smiles and great interest rushed to help him up, fussing over him, offering him water, coffee, tea.

"Your grandfather is such a wonderful man," gushed the Etro lady as she handed back my credit card.

"He's not my grandfather," I told her, with a mischievous look.

She raised an eyebrow, but I didn't bother to explain.

Edward and I parted in the middle of the makeup and perfume bazaar on the main floor of Saks. He was off to Citarella to buy squid. He had promised to cook stuffed squid "Lisbon-style" for our next dinner, and he was keen to go early to the market before they sold out of their day's supply of baby squid. Full-grown squid wouldn't cut it.

"They're not tender enough," he said, winking.

I watched Edward skillfully weave his way through a crush of holiday shoppers and young, beautifully dressed men and women holding up bottles of fragrance. And I found myself smiling. Joy, happiness—it snuck up on me every time I saw Edward. In spite of everything that was going on in my life, I smiled.

At that moment, I was the luckiest woman on earth. I had bought a dress that wasn't exactly Cinderella's ball gown but that seemed to transform me nonetheless. Maybe the saleswoman had it partly right—Edward could indeed be my grandfather, but really he was more like a fairy godfather. In any event, he was looking out for me.

And I was now also looking out for him. It didn't feel like an obligation. I enjoyed calling him, having dinner with him, and in the process I discovered a brave new world. I became obsessed with food and wine—the macarons from Ladurée on Madison Avenue, the French sheep's milk cheese from an East Village shop, Italian truffle salt, the pink Portuguese vinho verde that Edward loved. Everything I found, I brought to Edward, who more than appreciated my enthusiasm.

I was still smiling when I followed a short distance behind Edward to the door, just to make sure he was OK. Then I watched as he headed up Fifth Avenue and disappeared into the holiday crowds.

6

Stuffed Baby Squid "Lisbon Style"
Salad with Homemade Vinaigrette
Cantaloupe, Coffee Ice Cream
Sauvignon Blanc

Don't tell Valerie," said Edward, passing me a steaming plate of squid, bubbling in a delicately spiced tomato sauce and stuffed with rice, celery, thyme, and . . . I couldn't place the other ingredient.

"Leeks?" I asked, after the first bite.

"No, scallions," he said.

I complimented him on the squid and told him that my mother was the only other person I knew who had made squid in a similar way. I had assumed that it was an old family recipe, passed down to my mother from my grandmother. But Edward's execution of the dish, even holding the bulging stuffed squid bodies in place with toothpicks at either end, took me back to my childhood.

Like Edward's Paula, my mother had recently passed away and I felt her loss keenly. On some days, I made a mental note to call her, only to realize seconds later that she wouldn't be picking up the phone.

"Where did you get the recipe?" I asked in astonishment.

He brushed off the question. "Oh, Is-a-bel . . ." he smiled. He enunciated each syllable when he wanted to convey something that should have been obvious to me or to suggest that he really had no intention of giving me an answer. In moments such as these, I felt my mother's presence in an elemental embrace. Maybe it was the intimacy it signaled. On some level, Edward had taken over the parenting that I was now missing.

Focusing on the odd coincidence of the squid, I almost forgot what Edward had said about Valerie. "Don't tell Valerie" was a phrase he repeated often, especially when he was embarking on what might be considered a foolhardy venture, something he was convinced his younger daughter, my friend, simply wouldn't understand.

This time he didn't want Valerie to know about the poetry he submitted to the literary journals. Edward was certain his work would never be published, anyway. But perhaps he held out a faint hope that someday someone besides his family might appreciate the sentiment, the artistry of what he labored over at his little wooden desk and the dining room table on the nights that he desperately ached for Paula. Even though Valerie typed his poems for him, I'm sure she never imagined that he was submitting them for publication.

Usually when he received the typed verses, he couldn't deal with seeing his words so neatly printed and divided into precise columns on the page. He told me that the poems, in their conservative font on bright white paper, suddenly looked sterile to him. So he made photocopies of the typed poems, cut out each line, and then reassembled them like a puzzle, gluing them onto a piece of paper, until he was satisfied that the indentations were right, that the spacing was a signal to breathe in the right places.

He wrote his poetry to be read aloud, with just the right pauses and inflection, and he practiced often. Edward confessed that he sometimes fell asleep reciting the poetry, practicing the rhythm, experimenting with intonation.

When sleep completely eluded him, though, he got up in the wee hours to write letters to Paula.

He encouraged me to do the same, to write letters to the dead, in my case my mother, telling her how I was really feeling about life without her. One afternoon, when I was particularly upset, I took Edward's advice and was startled by the result. When I sat down to write to my mother in a notebook, sadness spilled out of me. And once it was out in the open, I could no longer keep it under wraps.

"I never imagined that I would feel your loss so profoundly," I wrote to my dead mother. "I have never felt so alone."

My mother died shortly before I moved to New York, while I was spending some time in Brazil researching a book. A week before she died, she had called me and seemed very animated, asking how my research was progressing and delighted that eight-year-old Hannah, whom I had brought along, was picking up some Portuguese. I handed the phone to Hannah so that she could speak to her grandmother. Shortly after she hung up, Hannah broke into hysterical sobs.

"Nana's going to die," she said, inconsolable.

"Of course she's not going to die," I said, to reassure her. "She was so happy on the phone."

A week later, my mother had a stroke and went into a coma. She never recovered and I never could fathom why my daughter had had such a startling premonition. Perhaps my mother was the one who had had the premonition and that call, made while she was still full of life, was her way of saying goodbye to both of us.

In many ways, Edward reminded me of my mother. They both faced life with a cheerful equanimity. It took a lot to dispel their even tempers, although I saw them both get angry when they felt I was being threatened or taken advantage of. Edward and my mother were alike in other regards, too. They proved extremely well organized about cooking and death.

My mother pressed jars of her homemade vegetable soup on my brother and me when we were living on our own. She organized family feasts at Christmas and on our birthdays. She froze stock and the almond biscotti and lemon pound cakes she made from scratch. And, like Paula, she quilted pillows and bedspreads from the fabric remnants of old clothes.

I am ashamed to admit that I often balked at the soup

jars and the packages of parchment-wrapped frozen cake ("You can have it later," she would say), seeing them as parental interference when I was trying so hard to be independent. And I had little patience when later in her life she insisted on telling me about the plans for her own death. A devoted Catholic, she did not fear death. "I've lived a very good life," she said, when she turned eighty. Two months later she was gone.

A few years before my mother died, she and my father bought a plot under an oak tree in a park-like cemetery in central Toronto. On one of my visits home, she took me on a tour of where she would be laid to rest. The funeral mass would be at St. Mary's, the church she first attended with my father when they arrived from Portugal in the 1950s, she told me. It made her happy knowing that my brother and I would never have to worry about arranging a funeral.

When I told Edward the story of my mother's end-of-life preparations, he completely understood and related to me his own plans, even though he was now fulfilling his final promise to Paula and was no longer in a hurry to die.

Edward had divided Paula's ashes into three vases. He gave two of them to his daughters. He keeps his share of the ashes in an elegant Tiffany vase in his bedroom. He has told me that when he dies, he doesn't want a funeral. He wants to be cremated, his ashes mixed with Paula's in a Bloomingdale's brown shopping bag, and sprinkled throughout Central Park, which was their favorite place in the world. It's against the law to spread human remains in New York City parks, but Edward is sure he has that technicality covered. That's where the Bloomingdale's bag comes in. Who would ever suspect what the brown bag actually contained? Edward is an atheist, but he had no problem believing that he would be reunited with Paula and revisiting their favorite haunts—their ashes flying across the Great Lawn, up the turrets of Belvedere Castle and over the Reservoir and the manicured gardens of the East Side.

While he was not shy about broadcasting his own plans for death, he swore me to secrecy about his poetry. He also wanted to make sure that I hadn't told anyone about our shopping trip to Saks. It was only months later, when Valerie saw me applying a coat of particularly red lipstick on one of her trips to New York, that I really understood Edward's furtiveness.

"I'm going to wash that right off," said Valerie. I'm

not sure she would like it if I told her I might be turning into something of a femme fatale—and at the direction of her father. She thought her father's views on women were anachronistic, mired in a 1950s suburban utopia that saw women as stay-at-home moms.

"He can be rather controlling," she had said about Edward. I had no idea what she meant. But of course we all view our parents through our own particular lenses. I can remember being incredibly surprised when my friends told me that I had progressive parents. It's never how I would have described them. I saw them as conservative and strict with my brother and me.

Edward controlling? I felt Valerie's father was one of the most remarkable and evolved men I knew.

And Valerie was one of the most accomplished women I knew. She was brilliant and practical and extremely determined. She launched her career in publishing, after graduating from college in the late 1960s, by knocking on just about every publisher's door in Manhattan and boldly asking for a job. When I met her, she was already well established in her own firm. She gave me my first job when I was barely out of high school.

She still likes to tell the story of our initial meeting.

She and her business partner gave me a typing test as part of my interview for an internship in her office, which was located above an ice-cream parlor on a downtown street in Toronto. They escorted me over creaking floorboards to a back room, where there was a desk, chair, and an IBM Selectric typewriter. According to Valerie, I sat in the room for forty-five minutes before walking out, my footsteps loud on the old hardwood floors of the office. Valerie and her business partner looked up at me from the page proofs they were poring over.

"Um, how do you turn on the typewriter?" I asked.

I have only a vague, embarrassed recollection of the event, but Valerie says it was a decisive moment. "You're hired!" she says she said on the spot, although I think she must have given me the news in a phone call a few days later.

I spent my summer proofreading and was thrilled when I caught a mistake that the much more experienced copy editors had missed. "Desiccated has two *c*s!" I wrote triumphantly on a Post-it note one afternoon. I also read the piles of fat, unsolicited manuscripts that arrived in manila envelopes and were relegated to the slush pile. I went through each submission carefully and at first felt horrible about sending them back in the self-addressed stamped envelopes. But I soon grew adept at writing the perfect rejection letter, striking just the right balance between firmness and only slight encouragement on future endeavors. "Thank you very much for your submission... Unfortunately, your manuscript does not fit with our publishing program... Best of luck with your book..."

I worked two summers for Valerie. During that second summer she mentioned that her parents were visiting from New York City. She was marveling that her father was bringing her his Scotch broth. As a nineteen-year-old, I must have found the gesture both charming and bold because, decades later, I still remember it as something special. *What kind of person does this?* I thought. *He brought soup? How did he transport it from New York to Toronto? In a thermos?* It would be another twenty-five years before I would meet this somewhat peculiar and definitely wonderful man who transported soup over international borders.

Valerie, like her father, was a tremendous cook. When she retired from publishing, she bought a home in the country and grew her own vegetables and herbs. She cooked with edible flowers, made her own sorbet, experimenting with lavender, rosemary, and rose essence long before it was fashionable to do so. Years later, when I told her I was growing my own Swiss chard but didn't know how to cook it, she immediately suggested steaming it and then covering it in heavy cream, mixed with a teaspoon of Dijon and grated pecorino, before baking it in a hot oven. She suggested serving it over polenta, which I do now pretty much every time I have Swiss chard.

But while they shared many attributes, Valerie and Edward had many diametrically opposing views, especially when it came to women. Valerie had her mother's chestnut hair and confidence, her father's height and artistry. She wore elegant Armani suits, but she would not have reacted well to Edward's position on "feminine enhancement." After all, she seemed appalled by my Dior lipstick.

I wasn't about to tell Valerie about the shopping trip to Saks, nor about Edward's poetry submissions. In return, I believed we had an unspoken agreement: Edward was supposed to keep everything that was happening to me after I moved to Roosevelt Island to himself.

These were promises neither of us would be able to keep.

7

Bourbon
No ice
No tonic
No lime
Just neat

One Sunday afternoon, I showed up at Edward's apartment with a pound of raw squid from my favorite fish market in Newark. We both knew it was a pretext to visit him, and the tears started soon after I crossed the threshold.

He didn't seem at all surprised. "I wish there was something I could do to help you, darling," he said. "But if I interfere, it will just be worse for you."

"Friction, competition, confrontation, impatience,

and distraction." It was the first sentence of my horoscope for that weekend. The rest: "For the next few days you will have a shock. You are very sensitive in your relationships and everything will result in irritation. For this reason, it would be good to avoid complicated negotiations."

It was a Sunday morning, my husband and I were fighting, and in order to avoid "complicated negotiations" I had taken New Jersey Transit to the Ironbound section of Newark, the Portuguese neighborhood where I went regularly to buy salted cod and olive oil—the foods from childhood that made me feel grounded. I often took my daughter to a seedy barbecue joint on Ferry Street, the kind of place frequented by muscled cops and construction workers, that grilled chicken and ribs on charcoal. We would leave with our clothes infused with the smell of barbecue but satisfied with our meal of tender chicken, mounds of french fries, and a vinegary salad of lettuce, tomatoes, and bold slices of raw onion.

On this day I felt better after eating chicken at the Formica table of Ferry Street Barbecue and wandering the aisles of the nearby Portuguese supermarket, sampling olives, goat cheeses, and buying chorizo, but I knew I couldn't stay away forever. When I returned home the fighting started again. That's when I escaped to Edward's with my pound of squid.

Edward took the mollusks and stashed them in his refrigerator. Then he offered me a seat on his sofa, walked over to the hutch in his living room and divided the last of his Kentucky bourbon evenly between two glasses. He didn't bother with ice, or tonic or pastis, or even a squeeze of lime. He limped over to the sofa, shrugged his shoulders, smiled, and handed me my glass.

"How about a bourbon?"

He needn't have asked. I inhaled the soothing liquid heat and soon after that everything came pouring out of me. I told Edward about the horrible arguments, dishes crashing on the floor, a family dinner that became so bitter and nasty, my daughter left the table in tears and hid herself in her room.

"I'll never forget this dinner as long as I live," she cried. Nor, I thought, would I. But now on Edward's sofa I could no longer recall what had been so terrible that it resulted in platters laden with food being hurled across the dining room table and red wine splashed violently against a white wall, an appropriate abstract rendering of my marital discord that I hadn't bothered to clean up.

Perhaps it was a sign that our dysfunction was now alarmingly visible. The "melancholia," to borrow a nineteenth-century phrase the *New York Times* used to describe the maladies of patients shuttered in the asylum where we now lived, had been let loose within the confines of those walls. It was now sure to spill over to the outside world. Maybe friends had already noticed the sharp tones we used to address each other. At work, Melissa probably suspected. Why else was she so respectfully silent during my very uncomfortable phone calls home—conversations (could I even call them that?) that involved screaming on the other end and me trying unsuccessfully—in the middle of the newsroom—to calm the drama du jour in strained sotto voce.

In some ways, I identified with Nellie Bly, the investigative reporter who went undercover at my madhouse in 1887 and wrote a series of exposés for Joseph Pulitzer's *New York World.* After ten days at the psychiatric hospital, she documented forced meals of spoiled food and ice-cold baths where prisoners were required to stand in long lines and wash themselves in the dirty water left by their fellow inmates.

Bly wrote about how prisoners from the nearby

penitentiary even doubled as orderlies, keeping inmates in check through savage beatings. Among Bly's observations, recorded in her book *Ten Days in a Mad-House*, which I had recently read, "From the moment I entered the insane ward on the island, I made no attempt to keep up the assumed role of insanity. I talked and acted just as I do in ordinary life. Yet strange to say, the more sanely I talked and acted the crazier I was thought to be."

Well, maybe things weren't as bad as all that but, like Bly, I was an investigative reporter who had also entered The Octagon undercover—when we moved in I was pretending that everything was all right with my life. But as soon as I began to get a grip on reality and reclaim myself, "the crazier I was thought to be." When I brought up divorce with my husband, I was taken aback by his response. Was I mentally ill, menopausal? Had I had my thyroid checked lately? Perhaps I needed a psychiatrist, antidepressants? What about yoga? Bly's statement ricocheted through my brain.

I'm not sure I did a good job explaining any of this to Edward. On that fateful Sunday afternoon I spent a lot of time crying my way through the bourbon, sounding incoherent even to myself. Edward listened and, at one point, rose to refill our glasses, having forgotten that we had already consumed the last of the bottle. I looked out his living room windows at the lights in the buildings across the water. It was already dark and I knew it was time to go home. Even in my leave-taking, though, there was something comforting. I guess I knew that after the drama, Edward would always be there. As he escorted me to the elevator, holding the door open with his outstretched cane, he said, "Let's have dinner soon, OK?"

A couple of days later, I received a phone call from Valerie. Edward had told her everything about my crisis. She told me he was distraught, mostly because he felt there was nothing he could do to help me. As I listened, I became upset with myself for having put Edward under so much stress. "He's very worried about you," said Valerie.

But Edward never conveyed his worries to me. He never dwelt on my situation, rarely offered any specific marriage advice, never interfered. On occasion, he would sigh and shake his head. "It's a bloody shame," he would say, knowing that I was the only one who could solve my problems.

8

Beef with Sauce Bordelaise
Pan-Fried Potatoes with Gruyère
Salad of Mixed Greens with Homemade Vinaigrette
Apple and Pear Galette
Malbec

Edward was cutting beef into very thin slices with the precision of a surgeon when I showed up for dinner with a bottle of Argentine Malbec. He glanced quickly at the bottle and, surprisingly, decided that the wine would be excellent with his beef. He had already made the bordelaise sauce before I arrived, mixing a few spoonfuls of his demi-glace with wine, shallots, and butter. Now he piled the thin slices of meat on plates and spooned the sauce on top, finishing with slices of pan-fried potatoes coated in melted Gruyère.

We took our seats at the table, and Edward opened the Malbec. There was silence as he poured the wine. I knew that he wanted to ask me how things were going at home. It had been weeks since our sad cocktail hour, and I had put Edward off whenever he called to invite me for dinner. I was afraid to cause him any more concern than I already had.

But tonight, I had relatively good news to impart—my husband had finally agreed to a separation. Now the problem was that we couldn't get out of our lease without severe financial penalties. Neither of us could afford to leave The Octagon right away.

In the following weeks we began to stake out territory in the apartment, and carve out separate kingdoms. I barricaded myself in a bedroom or took over a spot on the sofa in the living room while he stockpiled an arsenal of once-shared belongings in his home office. He had laid claim to a mountain of books, dishes and our imported French pots, the plasma TV, and even cans and boxes of non-perishable food. At first, I considered myself above such pettiness, but I eventually worked up the nerve to seize the coffeemaker and the toaster only after Melissa urged me to snag what I wanted.

We cooked separate meals and were never in the kitchen together. We somehow managed to work out a schedule for spending time with our daughter. When he left to visit relatives in Canada, I breathed a sigh of relief and dismounted from the tightrope that had become my marriage, as if an enormous weight had been lifted off my back.

During this period of domestic détente, I also became an outcast among our neighbors. I joked to Edward that I had become the Hester Prynne of Roosevelt Island, or at least among the community of mostly Serbian émigrés we had befriended.

Before the decision to separate and get a divorce, I was affectionately known as "the foreigner" at neighborhood soirees. These were stilted social affairs at which men sat separately from women, drinking Scotch and *rakija* and singing lugubrious songs about exile from their homeland. Many had arrived in New York as refugees during the conflicts that had splintered the former Yugoslavia. They went on to work at the United Nations or build small businesses in Manhattan and Queens. Moving into government-subsidized apartments, they formed a community of some two hundred families. At first they welcomed us to their parties and barbecues because my husband was of Serbian origin and I had covered the Balkans as a foreign correspondent before we moved to New York.

After my husband informed them of our separation, I might as well have had a huge scarlet "D" for divorcée affixed to my back. I no longer received invitations to parties and some of the men of the community even refused to acknowledge me when I bumped into them on Main Street. The coup de grâce came when one of the mothers—a fifty-something homemaker fond of track suits—refused to allow her nine-year-old to have a play date with my daughter at our apartment.

It might not have been seventeenth-century Puritan Boston, but I had been formally expelled from the Serbian ghetto. Roosevelt Island became even more of a prison for me.

Back in the 1980s, for Edward and Paula, Roosevelt Island represented freedom, a ticket out of a different prison. Well into their seventies, they found themselves alone in a neat suburban bungalow on Long Island. Their daughters had moved out years before and they missed old friends and the places they loved in Manhattan. Paula did not drive and the prospect of living out their retirement in a far-flung bedroom community didn't appeal to either of them.

In the 1970s, architects and planners held Roosevelt Island out as an urban oasis with a small-town sensibility. It was conceived in 1969 when the state of New York entrusted the legendary architect Philip Johnson and his partner John Burgee to transform what by then was a derelict penal colony into a vibrant residential community for middle- and low-income families. They developed waterfront parks and hired modernist architects to build large apartments with spectacular views of the Manhattan skyline. In 1971, the island was grandly renamed after Franklin Delano Roosevelt, although New Yorkers still referred to it by its derisive 1920s moniker, Welfare Island.

Paula and Edward didn't care. When they made their move back to New York, their old haunts near Washington Square and Greenwich Village had become too pricey. The island seemed like a safe and affordable alternative, and they soon settled into an agreeable routine. Edward walked to Astoria over the Roosevelt Island Bridge, where he patronized a small network of food purveyors—a fishmonger who called him with news of a shipment of Hudson River shad, a butcher who saved him ham bones for stock. When he wanted to go into "the city," as islanders referred to Manhattan, he squeezed into the tram, then journeyed by foot the more than sixty blocks to Chinatown for the duck he liked to use in his cassoulet and to the French butcher in Chelsea for the best merguez.

Although Edward and Paula were fully aware of the history of their new community, Roosevelt Island for them seemed to represent a much better life. They re-explored their beloved Manhattan and spent their last years together taking long walks through Central Park, dining at the Oyster Bar in Grand Central, attending the theater. In fact, they grew to prefer the island, where they soon became well-known among their circle of friends for their elaborate dinners. And everyone begged Edward for his apple galette. The handwritten Thanksgiving menus I found in his photo albums and scrapbooks always featured Edward's signature dessert.

He insisted that the secret was crushed ice, even after my complaints. Crushed ice, he repeated. And lard. Tonight at dinner, after we finished the galette, Edward got up from the table, gathered his cane that was draped on one side of his dining room chairs, and walked slowly to the refrigerator. He opened the freezer, took out a rectangular brick of white lard, wrapped carefully in waxed paper, and presented it to me with a flourish.

"Voilà," he said.

I was so touched, seeing in Edward's gift such kindness, and even meaning. I lingered, slowly pulling on my heavy coat and boots. Outside, a storm seemed to be winding down, but I wasn't looking forward to the cold trek to my apartment. At the elevator, Edward kissed me goodbye and said simply, "I hope you're happy, darling."

I trudged through the newly fallen snow, past the silent communal garden and The Octagon. I walked with purpose even as I had no real sense of where I was going until I reached the northernmost point of the island and the Gothic lighthouse, surrounded by the churning waters of Hell Gate. Although it was built in 1872 by James Renwick Jr., who would go on to design St. Patrick's Cathedral several years later, local legend has it that the inspiration for the lighthouse actually came from one of the patients at the insane asylum.

John McCarthy feared a British invasion, and the diligence with which he began constructing a fort so impressed his minders at the asylum that they allowed him to finish what became a four-foot clay structure, perhaps believing that it was a good form of therapy. For me, the late night visits to the lighthouse had also been therapeutic. As on so many previous occasions, I headed to my usual bench with its view of Manhattan across the river.

But something had changed tonight.

It was still snowing lightly, but even the waters of Hell Gate seemed calm. I was alone, on the snowy banks of the river. In the silence immediately following the storm, the lights of the Upper East Side and Harlem seemed to grow brighter. Without any real sense of why I was doing it, I stood up, took out my iPhone, inserted my earphones, and scrolled through iTunes until I found a samba.

Suddenly, I was immersed in Afro-Brazilian drumming. I began to move my feet, hesitantly at first, and then the samba just *spilled* out of me, and I felt my soul move—in my hips, my stomach, my feet, my ass.

I wanted desperately to call Edward, to shout, "Yes!"

into the phone. But it was late, and Edward was probably already asleep.

And, anyway, he knew. "I hope you're happy, darling" contained no question mark. In my mind, there was no punctuation at all. It was a floating affirmation, as simple and as complex as smiling.

9

Oysters Rockefeller
Avocado Salad with Homemade Blue Cheese Dressing
Tarte Citron
Pinot Blanc

My transformation didn't happen overnight. It was gradual. I still took the lonely walks along the East River, but now I plugged headphones into my phone and began to listen to music. I went to parties, to the theater. I ran six miles a day, and I started to reread the poetry I had once loved as a university student.

The world is charged with the grandeur of God.
    It will flame out, like shining from shook foil;

It gathers to a greatness, like the ooze of oil
Crushed.

"The grandeur of God?" I don't know if I shared poet Gerard Manley Hopkins's religious convictions. If I believed in anything during those years, it was the grandeur of dinner. I believed in the magic of Edward.

My job also buoyed me. When I first arrived I was unschooled in the world of New York tabloids. When my editor told me to go out and "get a wood," I had no idea that it was slang for the front-page story. Nor did I understand when he sent me on a "door knock," by which he meant an ambush in which you arrive without warning and knock on the potential interviewee's door. I also had no idea how to proceed when he barked, "Look for more johns." But I quickly got the hang of it.

On occasion, Melissa and I bitterly complained about our circumstances at work, both of us veteran reporters approaching middle age and the respectability that was supposed to attend that, but didn't. Mostly, though, we shook it off, drawing some kind of reassurance that no one else was given any kind of special treatment at the paper. We sought ways to make our workdays more enjoyable.

We took solace in our mutual love of food, taking turns buying Petrossian croissants—fat, chewy, and buttery—whenever we had to go on a stake out. When on assignments in Flushing, Queens, we conducted "source" meetings at Joe's Shanghai so that we could order the soup dumplings—pork meatballs encased in delicate little pagodas of white dough, steaming from the broth. We picked up tuna sandwiches—on thick slices of freshly baked, crusty rye bread, with finely chopped iceberg lettuce and tomato slices—from a Westchester deli when we were in the area. It was unlike any other tuna sandwich I'd had, and I am not sure if it was because it was truly great or because food just tasted better outside the newsroom, where on many days we ate three meals at our desks piled high with documents, which, in my case, intermingled with crumbs, stray pouches of Heinz ketchup, and old paper coffee cups.

Melissa's desk was, if not quite pristine, always better organized and definitely cleaner than mine. She kept a bottle of hand sanitizer near her computer, and used it several times a day. She had a stash of alcohol wipes from the first aid kit in the newsroom's small kitchen to wipe off the earpiece on her phone. She did this if I happened to be coughing and had borrowed her phone.

We were both devoted to our work. The first time we wrote a groundbreaking front-page story involving shady politicians in Queens that sparked multiple federal investigations, our editors took a page out of *All the President's Men* and began calling us Klincent—an amalgam of our last names, Klein and Vincent. Bob Woodward and Carl Bernstein, the *Washington Post* journalists who brought down President Richard Nixon with their reporting on Watergate, were famously known in their newsroom as "Woodstein" and did most of their work as a team.

I often joked with Melissa that she could be the female equivalent of Woodward, tall and patrician with a neat desk and proper files, as played by Robert Redford in the movie. Like Woodward, she also did all the driving in her old but clean Honda. Of course, she pegged me as Bernstein, played by a young, disheveled Dustin Hoffman—tortured, disorganized, brimming with outlandish ideas for stories that more often than not stretched her patience.

After a hard day's work, it was especially heartening

to know that at least once a week Edward and dinner were waiting for me. Today, whenever I describe my life on Roosevelt Island, I talk about it as the worst time of my life. But I would be lying if I didn't tell you it was also the best time. Because of Edward.

One night when I arrived for dinner, he was preparing oysters Rockefeller.

"What's the occasion?" I asked as he arranged the oysters on a baking dish and topped them with a mixture of spinach and bread-crumbs sautéed in butter and Pernod.

"Do we need one?" he replied, the slight lilt in his voice indicating that I had asked a silly question. "Paula and I never needed an occasion," he continued. "We never gave each other presents, either, because every day we spent together was a gift."

I imagined that Edward had lived some kind of fairy tale with Paula—a relationship so rare and fantastical that it could surely never happen to me, or anyone else I knew. At first, it might have seemed an unlikely match. He was a Southern boy, raised in genteel poverty, and she was an urbane Jewish intellectual from Philadelphia, five years his senior. But, as Edward remembered his first glimpse of Paula, it was love at first sight when they met in 1940 at a Greenwich Village theater—both of them aspiring actors, hoping to land a role with the Provincetown Players.

The group's playhouse, in a brownstone on MacDougal Street, had been set up in 1916 by some of the original founders who had started the company during their summer vacations in Provincetown, Massachusetts. Early members included Eugene O'Neill and the poet and journalist John Reed. Although the founding group had largely disbanded by 1929, the theater was still known for independent, experimental productions when Edward knocked on its door. But he clearly had more than acting on his mind. During that first tryout, he found himself auditioning for an audience of one—the tall, brown-eyed actress he had seen when he first walked in.

Paula had come to New York to be an actress, although her day job was painting cheap jewelry in a factory. She loved to be onstage, both inside and outside the theater. She enjoyed pranks. Sometimes she would tell people that she had grown up in China, the child of missionaries; other times, that she was a secret agent.

Edward also dreamed of the stage. At 19, he arrived

in New York City on a sweltering day in late August, stiff and sweaty from the trip sandwiched between two beefy and seemingly immobile passengers in the backseat of the car that brought him from Nashville. Years later, when he told me about his two-day ride, he could still remember driving through the Holland Tunnel "in amazement," patting his jacket pocket where he had stashed the envelope with a recommendation letter and $12—the equivalent of about $200 today—from his high-school drama teacher. In the letter, she praised his acting in the school production of *Death Takes a Holiday*, and she had given him the money toward his new life in the Big City.

Edward was determined to become an actor in a place that back then was still considered foreign and exotic to many Southerners, an American Babel. "All we knew about New York at that time was that there were people from all over the world who all spoke different languages," he said. "It might as well have been a different country."

Edward's mother had arranged for him to stay with a man she had once done business with in the South. His name was John, a German émigré who lived at University Place and Eighth Street. Edward rang his doorbell at 12:30 the night he arrived but there was no answer. Which is why he decided to settle into an armchair in the lobby of the nearby Lafayette Hotel and, before he knew it, he awoke at daybreak.

Edward returned to John's studio apartment, and this time the wiry, red-faced man opened the door. It would take a month of sleeping on John's daybed but finally Edward secured his own place on the second floor of a MacDougal Street tenement where he was to be the building's superintendent. The job entitled him to free rent and he could make his own hours. Now, he would have his days free to work with *real* actors. And on that first day at the Provincetown, he met the woman of his dreams.

Eager to impress Paula on their first date, he went shopping for a bottle of wine. He couldn't afford the French wine that a salesman suggested and ended up buying "the sweet wine that the bums on the Bowery drank." He didn't own any wine glasses; on that romantic night they clinked coffee cups.

"I asked her if she wanted to sleep over, and she said 'yes,'" Edward told me matter-of-factly. To my mock-shocked expression, he explained, "I had two beds and I was damned if I was going to let her sleep alone, so I crawled in beside her." They soon became inseparable, eagerly planning their lives together over the 50-cent plates of Chinese food at the Dragon Inn in the Village and on long walks in Central Park.

Several months later, when they decided to try their luck in Hollywood, Paula insisted that she travel to California as an honest woman. "Our intention had been to marry at city hall but when we tried to take out the license several days before, Paula's birth certificate showed her name as 'Pearl' and the bureaucrats said no dice. Not the same person." So, the day before their trip to the West Coast they went from church to church in Manhattan, hoping they could convince someone to marry them in a hurry. The pastor at Trinity Church in lower Manhattan agreed, but could they come back in a month? Edward took Paula's hand and they returned to the Village, determined to get married that afternoon.

It happened at the Washington Square Methodist Episcopal Church on West Fourth Street across from Washington Square Park and around the corner from the Provincetown Playhouse, where they first met.

"On November 8, 1941, Paula and Edward were married in this church," reads the index card next to a yellowing newspaper photo of the Washington Square Church in Edward's scrapbook. Their friend Lenny Black served as best man. Before the ceremony, as he waited with Paula and Lenny at the entrance to the church, Edward debated how much he was going to pay the pastor to perform the service. Edward sheepishly asked if he would accept $2.

"I'll accept whatever you're willing to give," said the pastor, who didn't ask any questions of the young couple.

A few minutes later the chords of Mendelssohn's "Wedding March" boomed throughout the Romanesque Revival building. "Paula and I both cried, maybe with relief," wrote Edward on the index card next to the only photograph of their wedding. Both Paula and Edward are beaming in the black-and-white picture. Edward wore his only suit. Paula sported a fitted, knee-length peplum plaid dress borrowed from her friend Mitzi. "It was red," said Edward.

Later that day, they stopped in Philadelphia on their way to California to visit Paula's parents. Then Lenny and his friend Mac drove them in Lenny's beat-up Dodge to the West Coast. On the first leg of their journey they stopped at Front Royal at the foot of the Blue Ridge

Mountains. At the modest tourist home, all four of them spent the night in one room with two double beds.

"I made love to her," said Edward, smiling at the memory of his crowded wedding night. "I don't know what Lenny and Mac did, but I couldn't wait to make love to her."

After a few moments of reflection, his blue-gray eyes growing shiny with the beginning of tears, he returned to preparing the oysters. "She melted my heart," he said. "Paradise was me and Paula."

As we sat down to eat Edward's oysters Rockefeller—a riot of green served on the craggy half-shells—I moved the bottle of wine and reached over the breadbasket to squeeze his hand.

I THOUGHT I HAD found paradise, too. It was on the old Constantinople road between Belgrade and Pristina, as I was making my way to Kosovo, weeks before the NATO bombing of the former Yugoslavia. My companion—the man who would become my husband—was a war photographer, as addicted as I was to the adrenaline rush, the excitement mixed with the utter sense of dread that comes from negotiating your way through a guerrilla checkpoint using nothing more than charm and a pack of Marlboros.

We drove in a clunky, rented Hyundai, so wrapped up in each other that we seemed oblivious to any danger, even as the car caught fire just outside Kosovo's capital. In Pristina, blackbirds sang at night amid the crackle of gunfire and swarthy mobsters in black leather jackets swarmed the bar of the Grand Hotel, which seemed forever enveloped in a cloud of smoke. I am convinced our daughter was conceived in one of that establishment's luxury suites, where the walls were punctured with bullet holes and the floors were littered with the cigarette butts of previous guests.

By the time NATO bombs started falling on Serbia in the spring of 1999, I was too pregnant to travel. For the sake of the baby, we decided we'd had enough of international conflict. But a normal life with a backyard, trips to Home Depot, and family barbecues seemed to elude us. Restless, we eventually found ourselves driving through the Holland Tunnel on a blustery day in February when my daughter was eight years old.

Like Edward more than half a century before, I drove through that tunnel in amazement. I was determined to make my way as an investigative reporter in New York City, a place I'd loved since I was a teenager obsessed with Woody Allen and F. Scott Fitzgerald. I'd longed to work at a New York daily, imagining myself as the tough-talking star reporter Hildy Johnson with the stylish, boxy 1940s suits, working for a Cary Grant-like editor á la *His Girl Friday*.

That's how I pictured it, anyway. I had no idea how hard the job would be or that life as a reporter at the *Post* would present its own set of challenges. Still, when it comes to work, I have no fear of seeking out the truth. My personal life is another matter. I have always approached it as an afterthought, although looking back I don't think I ever thought even that much about it at all. In fact, when I found myself mechanically reciting "I dos" and "I wills" before a justice of the peace at Toronto's city hall, it was a purely bureaucratic decision. In order to take up residence in New York, we all needed to travel under my immigration visa—an "O" given out sparingly to foreigners and referring to section 101 (O)(i) of the Immigration and Nationality Act, which provides for "aliens of extraordinary ability" to be admitted to the United States. The INS would not accept our common-law arrangement, and the only solution was marriage.

Which is how I found myself on a cold, gray February day at the Marriage Bureau, repeating my vows even as the signs of impending doom were everywhere. I wore black for the occasion, and the groom smirked—I thought he was just nervous—throughout the ceremony. Later, he confessed to me that he felt his life had been ruined. Maybe he suddenly felt trapped, unable to continue the peripatetic life of a photojournalist. Was there a tearful breakdown when I heard this? I can't remember. I think I simply shrugged and bulldozed ahead.

In the end, marriage really killed the relationship. It always does.

Years before, I had married my college boyfriend in a city hall ceremony, against the better judgment of just about everyone I knew.

He was an earnest English major from the Midwest whose purity of spirit and earnest manner I cherish still. The marriage was my idea. His Canadian student visa was expiring and marriage was the only way for him to continue to live in the country. On my twenty-second birthday—a gray, bitterly cold day in February—we repeated our vows before heading off to a local pub to watch the America's Cup final. He was a sailing fanatic and refused to miss the race. On our honeymoon we went to Quebec

City, where I was bitten by a stray dog. I spent my first weeks as a newlywed getting a series of rabies vaccines ordered by the Canadian health authorities.

The marriage ended several years later, as inauspiciously as it had begun, in a government office in Rio de Janeiro where we were working as foreign correspondents. We both showed up at the Canadian consulate, a high-rise with stunning views of the Atlantic Ocean and the sunbathers on Copacabana Beach. We signed our separation agreement under a Canadian flag and a photograph of Her Royal Highness Queen Elizabeth II, somber in her diamond tiara and lace gown. Maybe it was my imagination, but I detected a hint of disapproval in her forced smile.

Edward smiled when I told him the story of that first marriage and divorce, as I buttered a piece of baguette and took a forkful of his delicious avocado salad. I was relieved. I had told few people about it, fearing their judgment, embarrassed that I had treated marriage as a legal convenience rather than a magical union predicated on love. But Edward surprised me when he launched into a discourse on the meaning of love. He had done this before, emphasizing that I should never forget that romantic love is a practical exchange, a transactional agreement, and that attraction almost never lasts.

"Attraction is the beginning, but who can predict where that will lead? Or when it will end?" he said. "In fact, do we ask such basic questions? Seldom, if ever."

"Life's needs met life's needs," he had written in a poem, which he had sent me, about his first sighting of Paula. He repeated the line now.

"Give of yourself, not yourself," he continued.

I told Edward he wasn't being entirely honest about the practicality of attraction. I reminded him that on other occasions, after a tumbler of whiskey and a glass of wine, perhaps, the meaning of love took on a greater urgency, suffused with passion, desperation, even.

"Is there someone who will stand naked with you in the shower and hold you and comfort you?" he had once said in a hoarse whisper, his words seeming to tumble over one another. "If you can't do that with the person you're with, then you're not really in love."

The truth is Edward was preoccupied with defining love. I never understood if he was doing this for my benefit, or if he was somehow trying to come to grips with the very special relationship he'd had with Paula. Every morning, when he sat down to his coffee, scrambled eggs, and toast slathered with butter and apricot preserves, Edward went through a few pages of the dictionary, working alphabetically, searching for words that added to his compendium of love. He began with "admiring," moved on to "adoring," and the last time I checked, he hadn't progressed much beyond the *c*'s—"caring" and "cherished."

"You make a mistake if you don't try to figure out love," he said now as he served the *tarte citron*—boldly tangy with a hint of sweetness held in his feathery pastry. "If you give yourself to someone without understanding it, you are only asking to be a slave."

A few days later I found a four-page letter in my mailbox. "What is love? Like the majority of us you struggled to supply an answer, for the very simple reason that we seldom attempt to define it, even less to comprehend it," Edward wrote. "Love is being, not belonging. Giving and receiving, not possessing."

I'm not sure I fully understood what he was telling me. But there was something beautiful about the fact that Edward was exploring the meaning of love.

• • •

On New Year's Eve I had finally picked up my dress from Saks in the package room of my apartment building. I had been invited to a party. I would go unescorted, but as I put on my dress, I suddenly felt foolish. I was going to lose my nerve. I resisted the temptation to ring in the new year alone, curled up on the couch with a book or watching the crowds watching the ball drop in Times Square on television.

I stopped by Edward's apartment, partly to show off the dress he had picked out. The door was ajar, and I let myself in. Edward seemed tired and was slumped in a chair in the living room. It was just after eight in the evening, but he was clearly exhausted. The apartment was unusually silent—no jazz came out of the living room speakers, no cheery French songs that he liked to sing along to, mangling the words because he had never had the opportunity to learn the language. There was only the eerie howling of wind outside his windows.

But my arrival seemed to give him purpose, and he was all business by the time I took off my coat.

"Turn around," he ordered, and steered me to the mirrored wall in his dining room. First, he told me my earrings were all wrong. Then he was troubled by my hair. "On the left side, you need to put it behind your ear, and on the right, let it drape down your face," he said, fixing my hair the way he wanted it to look. "Don't keep pushing it back."

He looked me up and down, told me to remove my watch—"It's too distracting"—then grabbed his cane and limped into his bedroom to rummage through Paula's old jewelry box. He came back a few minutes later with a necklace, a bold, brown, enameled choker that had been one of Paula's favorites, he said.

"There." He stepped back and assessed me. "You look smashing!"

I stood in front of the mirror, looking at myself. The necklace was indeed perfect, the hair was just as Edward had ordered, and even the Dior lipstick, which I had applied earlier, looked natural to me. I was beginning to recognize this new woman I had become.

I caught sight of Edward behind me, looking admiringly—his project, his Eliza Doolittle finally transformed into a proper lady.

"You know, Edward, one day I hope I am lucky enough to meet a man just like you." I addressed his image in the mirror.

Edward seemed startled and suddenly he blushed with nothing to say. Our eyes met in the mirror, and there was a long silence. "I wouldn't want you to be late for the party," he finally said. Slowly, he helped me on with my coat, grabbed his cane, and walked me silently to the elevator.

"Happy New Year!" I said, as the doors burst open.

"Pump yourself up, kid," he said. "You've got a lot going for you. A lot on the ball.

"And," he paused, reaching over to smooth my hair. "Knock 'em dead."

10

Pan-Fried Cod on Steamed Spinach
Fresh Tomatoes with Homemade Pesto
Fleur de Sel Caramels
Turkish Coffee
Pinot Grigio

Edward served up the imported fleur de sel caramels with a flourish.

"They were sent from Megan," he said, fixing me with a momentous expression to make sure I had understood.

We had just finished a simple meal, by Edward's standards: Fresh cod, lightly sautéed in olive oil, a splash of white wine, on a bed of steamed spinach, sliced tomatoes with Edward's nutty homemade pesto.

Ella Fitzgerald sang in the background: "Oh, the shark has pretty teeth, dear; And he shows them pearly white . . ."

There was still a half bottle of pinot grigio on the table, and now he pressed Megan's caramels on me. They were "artisanal," each elegantly wrapped in silver cellophane. He had just received them in the mail.

OK, and just who is Megan?

Edward gave me a mischievous look. "You know you're not the only woman I write to," he said, with a wink.

I was taken aback. Could he be a little bit jealous? Was he feeling neglected that I had not been able to come over as often lately? I had been consumed with work, with finding a new place to live. The lease had finally expired on Roosevelt Island and I was thrilled to be moving back across the river to Manhattan. Of course it also meant that I probably wouldn't be seeing Edward as often.

So maybe I was the one who was jealous. I knew that Edward had other women friends, but I thought all of them were part of a couple—neighbors, mostly, whom he had known for years.

Megan was a foreign interest. Yet he must have told

me where he had met her, why they were corresponding. Maybe I had been so wrapped up in my move, sorting through the detritus of my marriage, packing boxes every day before and after work, that I hadn't paid that much attention. Suddenly I remembered that Megan was a graphic artist, that she was in her thirties. No doubt she found Edward charming.

Everyone did. Edward had no shortage of fans. There was Tad, the architect, who lived on Roosevelt Island. They had become so close that Edward once described him as the son he never had. Edward called him "darling," which is what he called all his good friends, male or female. He taught Tad to shuck oysters. Whenever he saw Tad, a stylishly bald middle-aged man with a cheerful disposition and a permanent five o'clock shadow, he kissed him on both cheeks.

"Remind me to teach you to shave, Tad!" he said, when he saw him at the small, community gallery that Tad ran on Roosevelt Island. Edward had taken me to the gallery to show off his own sculpture—a whimsical elaboration of human DNA that he had fashioned out of egg cartons and wire coat hangers.

"It's just something fun, to make you laugh," he said.

It was at the gallery, during another opening, that I was introduced to a couple, two men whom I had never met. Edward kissed both of them warmly. Edward was dressed in a cuffed white shirt and had on a tartan tie that he had fashioned from a ribbon that had once graced a Christmas present someone gave him. He wore a blue blazer and brown oxfords that he had polished until they shone.

"Edward's going to be the best man at our wedding!" gushed one of the men. They were going to be married at St. Mark's Church in the fall. I wasn't surprised that this ninety-three-year-old Southern gentleman was to have an important role at one of the first gay weddings in New York State history.

Nor was I surprised by the people Edward started inviting to our dinners, turning his living and dining rooms into an artistic and literary salon. He was definitely back in action now, having found the will not just to keep on living after Paula's death but to enjoy entertaining as well. On these occasions he called on me to act as his sous chef of sorts—the only times he allowed me to help him in the kitchen.

"You're not filling those plates properly," he scolded,

as I arranged lettuce and then spooned his homemade vinaigrette on top of the individual salad plates.

As usual, an eclectic and even odd group of people assembled around Edward's oak dining table. There was the sixty-six-year-old Czech artist, with the salt and pepper ponytail, and his American TV producer wife, who was some twenty years younger, with long, straight black hair and tight jeans. The artist had fled an oppressive Czech state and moved to New York in the 1970s. At one dinner, he told us that he had spent several years researching sex clubs in Manhattan for an art project. He said that during the UN general assembly, which had taken place a few days before, he had been invited to an event at which the Czech president had grabbed his wife's ass during the photo op.

Everyone laughed, except for the Albanian couple sitting next to him. They were immigrants from Montenegro and had arrived in the United States as part of a wave of refugees after the 1999 NATO bombing of the former Yugoslavia. They lived on the island, where they found themselves surrounded by Serbian neighbors. They said they didn't feel comfortable among them, that the ugly Serb nationalism that had fueled years of conflict in the Balkans had followed them to New York.

Then there was the dentist with the Long Island accent who had owned the pediatric dental practice on the ground floor of Edward's building, and still lived in an apartment there with his wife. Edward was often moved to invite them to dinner after meeting them in the elevator, the lobby, or the swimming pool.

One night the Czech artist told us he had cried the first time he had dinner at Edward's apartment. Maybe it was Edward's prime rib or the Grand Marnier soufflé he made for dessert, he said, but when Edward carved the roast the Czech artist was overcome with gratitude that such an elderly man was being so generous and that he had put so much time and effort into preparing dinner.

"I love entertaining," Edward had said.

Tonight as we enjoyed Megan's fleur de sel caramels, I realized that I wasn't the only single or devoted woman in his life. There was his next-door neighbor Suzanne, a milliner, who owned a tony boutique on Madison Avenue and was regularly invited to dinner. She often came with Rita. Rita was Tad's wife, but sometimes she came to dinner without her husband. A graphic artist who spoke with an exotic continental drawl, she would often swing by bearing exquisite chocolates, boxes of macarons or flowers for Edward. She sported a Louise Brooks bob and favored crisp, white, oversized linen shirts and big jewelry. She would head straight to the freezer to serve herself the martini that was always waiting there for her when she came for dinner. She poured the chilled cocktail into the icy glass that Edward had set aside.

"Oh, Edward, it's perfect," she would say, savoring the martini, while peeking under the lids of the pots that were simmering on the stove. "What did you cook for us tonight, Edward?"

Every year, Edward and Paula had spent Thanksgiving with Rita and Tad and their family on the island. He and Paula had treated the couple's two children like their own grandchildren. When Rita and Tad's daughter Eliza died suddenly of an aneurysm in her dorm room at college, Edward was devastated. Years later he still couldn't speak about her death without sobbing.

I thought back on how many other lives Edward had touched, people he had met in a seemingly random fashion—waiting for the F train, at a shoe store in midtown, at the counter of his local butcher, or even in a hospital room after a routine surgical procedure. Edward found people special and he had a unique ability to coax the most profound stories out of just about everyone he met. When I finally left Roosevelt Island, I missed being able to just drop by unannounced and hear a story about someone Edward had met. One night at dinner Edward told me the story of his Irish neighbor, another Megan, who had confessed to him at the butcher shop how she had stolen a shilling when she was a six-year-old living in poverty in Ireland. They were speaking about *Angela's Ashes*, and Megan was explaining to Edward how true to life Frank McCourt's book about poverty in Ireland really was.

"One day when I was a child, I went alone into the church," she told Edward. "I sat down in the middle of the pews and a lady I knew came in and walked to the altar rail." Megan went on to describe how the lady knelt and prayed and then lit a candle before dropping a coin in the offertory box but missing the slot. "I watched as it fell to the floor. It rolled and it rolled and it rolled and then it stopped." Megan went to pick up the coin.

"Did you put it into the offertory box for her?" Edward asked.

In what seemed like a momentous confession some fifty years after the fact, Megan was near tears when she told Edward that she had pocketed the coin. She bought a loaf of bread with the money. "And I've felt guilty ever since," she said.

Edward then asked her if she was a Catholic.

"Well, I was," Megan told him. "I'm not much of anything anymore."

Edward disagreed with her. She was still "under the influence" of the Catholic Church, "in a good and positive way."

"Under the influence, yes," she'd said to Edward. "I like that."

Edward was so moved by his encounter with Megan that he wrote out her story in longhand. When he felt it was good enough, he asked Valerie to type it.

Edward said that writing about people he encountered made him feel alive. He needed to record his experience, he said; it reminded him that he was still someone who could feel very deeply, even though he knew his life as he hit his nineties had become limited. He once confessed to me that he knew he would never be with a woman again, never feel a woman's body next to him in bed, legs entwined, arm around a firm waist, head resting on a warm shoulder. In a moment of intense despair, he told me that he now sought solace in a hot shower. He described the sensation of scalding water cascading over his arthritic hands as "orgasmic." Physical intimacy was in the past; Edward knew that, but he still lived intensely and he was determined to continue doing the things that made him feel alive and useful to others.

"When I met Paula, I didn't know any limitations about what I could accomplish," he told me now, after he served our coffee. "I was full of myself about my facility. I wasn't above grabbing the sheets off the bed and washing them by hand. When Paula saw me she said, 'Nobody does that.'" Before Edward, Paula had only met men who were "big talkers"—the kind of intellectuals who sat at Blenheim's cafeteria at Seventh Avenue and Fourteenth Street chain smoking and drinking cup after cup of coffee, talking about all the things they would do, but getting nothing done. Edward wasn't like that. He could build furniture, grow vegetables, tailor a suit.

And, as I had come to realize, Edward was still a man for whom nothing was impossible.

11

Shrimp and Corn Chowder
Mussels Rémoulade
Chocolate Cake, Buttercream Frosting
Muscadet

"I told them the truth: I was ninety-three, and I hadn't done this in twenty years," said Edward.

We were sitting at Edward's dining room table where he had set out two large bowls of creamy shrimp and corn chowder and thick slices of crispy baguette. Edward poured us each a glass of exquisitely dry muscadet, and immediately launched into his big news.

A while back Edward had taken on what appeared to

be an impossible task. He had agreed to re-upholster his neighbors' antique sofa. Perhaps he feared that his plan was half-cocked but, as he put it to me when I pressed him on why he would want to embark on such a huge task, he said, "Voltaire's prescription for avoiding suicide was work."

They had been reluctant even to ask, and it was Edward who had convinced Steve and Lenore to let him have a go at the sofa: "I told them I would try, and if I were successful they would save $3,000." He accompanied them to Zarin Fabrics on the Lower East Side, and together they sorted through bolts of rich brocades and silks. On days when his hands were swollen from arthritis and he could barely grip the shears to cut through the thick fabric, he slowed down. He took a day off. Or two. Sometimes three. But he never despaired.

As it was, I was having my own sofa problems. They occurred on the day I was moving out of the Roosevelt Island apartment and renting a tiny pre-war one-bedroom on Central Park South. I had reluctantly gone to see the apartment at the insistence of a friend who lived in the building. I feared that it would be too small for Hannah and me. The apartment, which overlooked the park, had been occupied by an artist for more than thirty years. She was relocating to the Midwest and needed to find someone to sublet it. Would I be interested?

I took it on the spot and couldn't wait to move in. The artist had used the tiny bedroom as a studio after her own daughter had left home. She stored her paintings and watercolors—some of them enormous twelve-foot-high canvases—in a sliding shelf she had fashioned in the larger room. The floor-to-ceiling shelf divided the space so that she had a private sleeping area, a desk, and a living room with a small dining table. The kitchen was miniscule and featured Formica counters and the original whitewashed cupboards.

"Living here will be good for you," said the painter, who was in her eighties, soon after I met her and agreed to help her pack up decades' worth of watercolors, dusty books, and antique silverware. It turned out we had a lot in common. She had moved into the apartment with her young daughter following her own divorce. She had derived much strength at the time from an elderly woman she had met while living in France and had gone on to write a memoir about the whole experience. When I blurted out some of the details of my own recent separation and friendship with Edward, she smiled and said confidently, "There are no coincidences."

I was starting a fresh life, and it was somehow appropriate that when I tried to cram the vestiges of my old one into my new apartment, they literally wouldn't fit. My sofa was large and what interior designers might call an "important piece." It was inspired by the Earl of Chesterfield, or that was the story the antique store owner spun when I admired the grand, carved mahogany armrests.

The sofa had been our first furniture purchase when I was still part of a couple, and we'd proceeded to replace the sofa's blue and white chintz upholstery with Hermes orange chenille and creamy ultra suede and goose down pillows. Restored to its former grandeur, it graced our homes in three cities, but by the time we separated, it had become an albatross around my neck. It was too big and too bulky to fit through the door of my new place.

When I moved I was separated but still enmeshed in a bitter legal battle, fighting what the clerks at the New York State Civil Supreme Court euphemistically called "contested matrimonial." It would be another year until I was officially divorced. My friends were stunned when I told them that I had landed an apartment across the street from Central Park in the grand art deco building that was Lois Lane's residence in the 1978 film *Superman.* In the movie, the superhero picks up the *Daily Planet* reporter from her rooftop terrace and takes her for a nighttime flight over the Statue of Liberty.

The building, a New York landmark, had also been home to the French aviator and writer Antoine de Saint-Exupéry, who lived there between 1941 and 1942 while he worked on *The Little Prince.* According to one of his biographers, Saint-Exupéry spent many hours on the rooftop terrace, dreaming of returning to his life as a pilot and launching paper planes into the park. I longed to do the same, daydreaming of paper airplanes flying from the rooftop over the taxis that sped along Central Park South and the green expanse that lay before me.

For hours, a crew of beefy men stacked cardboard boxes filled with books, dishes, shoes—all my worldly possessions—in the freshly painted living room of my new lodgings. They saved the sofa for last. It required four men to remove it from the freight elevator down the hallway. Straining and sweating under the weight of the large and unwieldy piece of furniture, they tried to angle the sofa several different ways to negotiate the threshold. But it would not fit, even after they removed the door from its hinges. Building superintendents were called in to oversee the delicate operation. The building manager came to give her advice. A small swarm assembled outside my door, and neighbors walking their dogs or returning from shopping were drawn to the crowd. There was talk of hoisting the sofa up through a window, but the windows were not large enough to accommodate the monster couch.

One of the building's handymen wanted to saw through the couch and disassemble it. But the sofa was so old that the foreman of the moving crew decided against it; if he allowed it to be taken apart, he might not manage to put it back together. This being New York, he was no doubt worried about potential liability involved in butchering an expensive antique.

I was losing patience and ready to junk the sofa, but my friend Zaba, who was helping me move and had watched the entire episode, was convinced it was too valuable to part with and suggested storage. So the moving crew lugged the piece back onto the freight elevator, packed it back into their truck, and drove it to a dusty warehouse facility in the Bronx, where it remains to this day.

After the sofa drama, everyone dispersed and I was left alone in my new apartment. In the stillness of that late summer afternoon, as the light poured into my apartment from the back window overlooking West Fifty-Eighth Street, I sat on the floor surrounded by piles of boxes. I felt very much alone and, I'm not ashamed to say, a little scared.

So I called Edward, who regaled me with the story of how he had spent the day tacking fabric onto his neighbors' couch. I can't remember if I unpacked my cooking utensils after I got off the phone with Edward. But I do know that the first room that I set out to organize was my sliver of a kitchen, with its window rattling from the churning industrial air conditioners one floor below. As pigeons alighted on the ledge, I started to cook.

I cooked that summer and into the fall. I stained my fingers purple peeling the beets that I turned into cold borscht. I chopped cucumbers and heirloom tomatoes that I bought at farmers' markets for gazpacho. When the air turned cooler I made stews with tiny green French lentils, fragrant with fresh thyme and bay leaves, which I served with seared merguez, crusty baguette, and a rich Argentine Malbec. I braised chicken in paper bags, à la Edward, I baked my mother's pound cake with sour cream and lemon zest, and I rolled buttery pastry dough between two sheets of parchment for Edward's fruit tarts. Sometimes, when I had leftovers, I took food into work.

"You're becoming my grandmother," Melissa said. "Stop pushing the food."

Shortly after I moved to my new apartment, Hurricane Irene hit New York City. The wind howled outside my window and the rain came down in sheets, but I slept through most of the excitement. The next morning, decked out in rubber boots and raincoat, I went in search of coffee. Everything was shuttered except the nearby Essex House Hotel, where scattered guests milled around the lobby staring at the rain.

I decided to survey the damage and sought out Zaba, one of my few Manhattan friends who owned a car. Zaba is a Polish-Argentine writer and former actress who had a stunning resemblance to Jeanne Moreau in her youth. She has lived most of her adult life in Manhattan, in a grand apartment filled with old family photos and the assorted bric-a-brac of her adventures around the world. A bird's nest she found in Central Park has pride of place on her artfully cluttered coffee table that also features seashells and a framed letter from the Argentine writer Jorge Luis Borges to her father, congratulating him on a fine interview. Zaba's father was one of Poland's greatest foreign correspondents and became the United Nations correspondent for an Argentine daily when the family moved to New York.

I spent many happy evenings listening to mournful Italian songs in front of a roaring fire, making space on Zaba's coffee table for the thin slices of serrano ham and manchego cheese that she loved to serve. She was usually game for anything. We once ended up the only women at a Yemenite restaurant in Brooklyn where we ate lamb that had been cooked underground in a terra cotta pot. If anyone would be up for driving through Manhattan in a hurricane it would be Zaba.

The next morning we drove through a surreal Manhattan, where sandbags lined the entrance to the Russian Tea Room on West Fifty-Eighth Street and skyscraper windows bore masking tape crosses. In Little Italy, hipsters waded through flooded streets. In Zaba's battered beige sedan, the passenger side-view mirror affixed with cellophane tape, we felt like an urban and slightly more bedraggled Thelma and Louise—windows open, our hair flying in the high winds, singing along to a scratchy Edith Piaf cassette: *"Non, rien de rien / Non, je ne regrette rien!"*

I reveled in a new sense of freedom, which now extended to taking my own liberties with Edward's recipes. When I made his scrambled eggs à la St. John, I added pieces of salty feta. Sometimes I'd stir in a tablespoon of red wine vinegar instead of milk or cream. But no matter what I added to the eggs, I never cooked them all at once. I did it in two steps, sometimes three, and they were always fluffy and perfect.

As I walked Manhattan and Queens in search of ingredients, I became quite particular, perhaps even more so than Edward. I argued with the staff at the small cheese boutique in the East Village—I needed the prosciutto di Parma to be parchment thin when they sliced it. I was even willing to leave the store if they refused to cut it to my specifications. You can't serve thick prosciutto; it defeats the point!

Had Edward created a monster?

I found merguez at Epicerie Boulud, the eponymous food store owned by French chef Daniel Boulud near Columbus Circle. The merguez was sublime, but I launched a mini revolution when they started to charge me tax on the sausage. I even wrote a story for the *Post* when they refused to comply with the New York State tax code that prohibits taxing raw food items. Despite the story and two visits from state tax authorities, who bought sausage undercover after my story appeared, Boulud wouldn't budge, insisting I was wrong. He later relented, admitted his folly, and called me to apologize for the tax on the merguez.

And I began to organize dinners for my friends. We crowded around the white "tulip" table that I had ordered on Amazon, laden with feasts inspired by Edward—chicken paillard, baked fennel sprinkled with pecorino, shrimp and corn chowder, apricot soufflé.

Although my new space was small in comparison to my old apartment, I realized that my life had grown much larger. I invited friends over for dinner on a regular basis. During my exile on Roosevelt Island, we almost never entertained. There was always an excuse—the apartment was never clean enough or my cooking was never up to the standards of the Serbian wives on the island, who prepared feasts of cabbage rolls and sweet crepes filled with preserves and topped with fine dustings of confectioners' sugar.

But I no longer compared myself to the hausfraus on Roosevelt Island. If I made mistakes, I didn't care. I was happy to cook and to entertain, and I now did so a few times a week. My apartment was open to everyone: my neighbors, my lovelorn single friends who came over to sip wine, and my daughter's school friends who, taking their cue from my newfound passion, cooked me a surprise birthday lunch of pasta with pesto and an arugula salad, complete with French vinaigrette and a glass of red wine.

One of my friends even proposed to his girlfriend on his way to my New Year's Eve soiree. Bob and Karen arrived beaming. Karen showed off her new diamond ring, and Bob sliced the loaf of bread he had baked for our dinner. We ate from a huge tray of salted cod and new potatoes—Hannah taking plates of food to her room to share with a friend who had come to see her Christmas presents. Bob and Karen had first met in high school in California, and had met up again in their sixties after both of their marriages failed.

Karen was a Manhattan art dealer who lived in an exquisite, art-filled apartment on Park Avenue. Bob, an engineer, had built his own house in a forest on the Pacific coast; he wove beautiful scarves and blankets on a loom; he made his own wine. When I first met him, he gave me a shawl he had woven for me and a dried butterfly—a symbol for the soul, he said. That same week, when I visited the Butterfly Conservatory at the American Natural History Museum, I was delighted when a butterfly landed on my shoulder. At that moment I felt blessed.

We toasted to Karen and Bob's engagement with the Veuve Clicquot that another friend had salvaged from a fashion shoot, and later we all headed up to the roof to watch fireworks exploding over Central Park. We hardly minded the cold winds that whipped against our faces as we gazed at the spectacular bursts of color lighting up the sky on the Upper West Side.

"I'll never forget this night as long as I live," said Karen. "It's magical."

Months later, on a summer night, tipsy on Albariño and munching on radishes topped with butter and salt, a group of us launched our own paper airplanes from the roof. We cheered them on, these lopsided and flimsy gliders that we had embedded with naughty messages. Some of them immediately nosedived onto the busy sidewalk below, but a few caught a breeze and were momentarily swept up before landing in traffic. None of them made it to the park, but we were undaunted, determined to practice folding sheets of paper until we made a plane that was so aerodynamically sleek that it would make it all the way into the park.

What would Saint-Exupéry have made of our rooftop efforts? No doubt he would have approved. As he wrote in *The Little Prince*, "It is only with the heart that one can see rightly; what is essential is invisible to the eye."

BUT ALL THAT WAS months in the future. Now, in his apartment, Edward poured more muscadet and we both finished our respective sofa stories.

Edward had successfully upholstered his neighbors' sofa. They were ecstatic and wanted to reward his kindness. He brushed them off, suggesting a bottle of single malt Scotch was payment enough. "I told them that if I was looking for gratitude it was under *g* in the dictionary," said Edward. "And if I were looking for validation, it was under *v*."

I picked at the last crumbs of chocolate cake on my dessert plate. Edward had made one of the lightest cakes I had ever tasted. He told me that he used egg whites beaten into soft meringue peaks to create the airy effect. Just then he strained to get up from his chair, even though the piece of cake that he had cut for himself lay untouched on his plate. No doubt he was preparing to kick me out. It was eight o'clock, after all, and he probably wanted to go to sleep.

But he surprised me. He went to the living room and brought out a black-and-white picture of Paula that I had never seen before. It was a portrait of his wife in her twenties, young, beautiful, self-assured, her shoulder-length chestnut hair coiffed like Hedy Lamarr's in *Algiers*. He'd captured the image with a $4 box camera shortly after their marriage. The faded photograph shows the much younger version of the woman with the raised chin in the color prints he has taped to the walls of his living and dining rooms.

"Paula had something; she had *lure*," Edward once told me. I immediately understood the significance of that word and that Edward had deliberately taken it from Cole Porter's "All of You," one of Paula's favorite songs, the one that she sang to him the day before she died. I saw that lure in this photograph. Edward had been wanting to frame it but had put it off. For months after her death, the picture lay among the stacks of letters, bills, and recipes that he wrote out in longhand on his little desk. When he had come upon the picture the week before, it didn't make him as sad as usual; he was finally inspired to frame it. He had taken it to a Staples across the river in Manhattan to buy matting. Now he told me what happened.

"Can I help you?" The clerk must have been in her twenties—tall, lithe, with thick brown hair framing fine features, smooth alabaster skin. Edward showed her the photograph of Paula and asked her to help him choose a mat.

"She's so beautiful!" said the young woman, staring at the portrait of Paula.

Encouraged, Edward almost forgot why he had come to the store. He launched into the story of how he had met his wife, the history behind the photograph, how he had taken the image on a beach in California when they both still believed that they could make it in Hollywood.

And then, sensing that the young woman had been unusually attentive—sensitive and beautiful and truly interested in his life—Edward asked her if she liked to read poetry.

"Oh, I love poetry!"

After he paid her for the mat, Edward wrote down the young woman's address, so that he could send her a few copies of his most recent poems in the mail. When he asked for her name, Edward's heart seemed to skip a beat when he heard the answer.

"Paula," she said.

12

Grilled Lamb Chops
Broccoli Rabe Stewed with Smoked Pigs' Knuckles
Corn Bread
Macarons
Malbec

I knew Edward was feeling nostalgic for the South when he called to tell me that he had been cooking a pot of broccoli rabe with smoked pigs' knuckles on the stove all day. He was also planning to make corn bread, he said. Would I please come to dinner? He knew it was an invitation I couldn't possibly refuse, but as I walked out of the subway and the few blocks to his building on Roosevelt Island, I wondered what had sparked the sudden nostalgia for his childhood in Nashville.

"Time is going by so quickly," he said, wrapping a dish towel around the hot plates of seared lamb chops, still sizzling from the grill pan.

I bit into pink flesh glistening with bits of fresh rosemary. The broccoli rabe was a deep green, slightly bitter and smoky, and so tender there was almost no need to chew—it simply melted on my tongue. The corn bread was dense and only a little sweet—a perfect counterpoint to the gaminess of the lamb and the smoky richness of the greens.

Dispensing with my utensils, I picked up one of my lamb chops with my hands and tore into the meat, gnawing it to the bone to savor every last bite. When I finally looked up from my plate, I told Edward that I agreed with him about how quickly time was passing. It had been more than three years since I met this endearing man. I was now officially divorced and my daughter was rapidly becoming a teenager.

But Edward shook his head. No, he said, he meant something else. He meant that he was conscious of time running out and that he just wouldn't have the energy to do some of the things he wanted to do before he died. He got up to clear the table.

He hadn't spoken about death for a long time. So what had changed?

Edward had gone to a funeral for a friend earlier in the week and his longtime doctor had died the day before. So death was on his mind again.

"When I die, I will probably have a memorial service, and I hope you will say something," he said in even tones. "You know so much about me."

Of course, Edward had already made it clear there would be no funeral for him. And he didn't want any memorial to be sad, or overwrought, certainly not religious. He admired the actions of his former physician. When Will Grossman was diagnosed with cancer and decided not to seek treatment, he wrote a letter to all of his friends, outlining what they had meant to him, and bidding them a proper adieu.

"He had great dignity," said Edward, who had started to write a poem about the doctor. For Edward, dignity meant someone who always seeks the truth and has integrity. And Will was clearly someone who stood out.

Edward had been attending a lot of funerals lately as his friends and family members steadily passed away. And he had been nothing but critical of most of the services. The funeral for his friend, Roosevelt Island neighbor Mike Michaels, who was ninety-one when he died, was an example.

"His family members got up to speak but they were too emotional," complained Edward. "That's not the way to honor someone's life or to tell a story."

So Edward, who was sitting in the back row, decided that Mike needed to be remembered a different way and asked the family if he could say a few words. Edward got up to speak in front of the sixty or so mourners, and after a few minutes had everyone laughing at the memory of a man who was the youngest in a family with five girls, whose Jewish parents were so grateful to have a boy that they always called him by the Yiddish term of affection *bubala*. For years, Edward told the group, almost no one in his family could recall his real name! Which is why he was known as Michael Michaels.

"All we have are our stories," said Edward.

I remembered something Rita had said at one dinner. "You know, Edward, I came for dinner, but I was really coming here for the story." We all came for the story. Edward was our own Scheherazade. At most of our dinners, there was a story Edward was burning to tell me. He spun tales about his life in the South, told me stories about the people in the portraits encased in silver frames on a shelf in his living room. There was an uncle who became a sugar baron in turn-of-the-century Cuba, a great-grandfather who had shot a man over land in Missouri and escaped to Mexico where he lived out the rest of his life on the lam, an aunt who had taken to the pulpit when her preacher father suddenly stopped talking in mid-sermon, overcome by throat cancer that constricted his vocal cords.

And now who would tell Edward's story? Would he simply be forgotten? I know these thoughts must have been occupying him. What would become of the voluminous scrapbooks in which he had so painstakingly chronicled that story—his life with Paula and his daughters? "What will happen to all these albums I have made with their personal importance? I wonder about that on occasion," he had once written to me. "But not for long, since it offers no resolution."

There were faded photographs of the neat house he and Paula moved into on Long Island after their first daughter, Laura, was born; of Edward and Paula on a trip to London; of Laura and Valerie graduating from high school; of family weddings. There was Edward standing proudly in his old living room beside a piece of furniture he had made, or next to the bushes of red raspberries in the backyard.

"We never had raspberries growing up, Dad," said Laura one night at dinner, after she had moved back to New York and settled into an apartment across the street from Edward.

Edward proved her wrong, by going back to the scrapbooks, dutifully examining every page to find the series of photographs Paula had taken of him in his garden. And there he was: a handsome, much younger Edward, proudly displaying his raspberry bushes in a color snapshot.

There were certain events in his past that he had longed to chronicle on the page, too, but while he seemed so adept at capturing the nuance in other people's lives, he had trouble writing about his own. Almost two years into our friendship Edward wrote me a letter about his struggles in making sense of his own story. He was specifically referring to the difficulty in writing about his father's death, an event that was still too raw to relate even more than half a century after the fact. Edward had sent me neatly typed copies of his stories, about his Irish neighbor Megan, about Paula, and many others, but he had never sent anything about his father.

"I have worked on it before, trying to get it down on paper, but each effort has failed. I gave up after trying to write it in the second person, to myself, as if I did not know it from having lived it."

But on this particular evening, after the lamb chops and the corn bread and the macarons that Rita had brought over from a Polish patisserie in Queens that afternoon, Edward swept aside our dishes with the back of his hand. He was determined to tell me the story, no matter how painful it proved to be.

In the summer of 1955, Edward's father lay dying in Nashville. Leslie was 68 and a lifelong smoker. He had been sick with cancer for a long time. Family members took turns watching him during the day while Veronica, Edward's mother, sold corsets to try to keep up with the mounting medical bills.

"After working all day long seeing people and selling, she came home to lie next to him in their small double bed," he said. "For sleep? For rest? For comfort? There couldn't have been much for her in those nights."

Veronica had Gibson Girl glamour, even after seven children, and even as she slid past middle age. In the sepia-toned portrait of his mother that he keeps in his living room, her brown hair is styled in a Victorian updo, with wispy curls touching the creamy skin at the nape of her neck. Edward was the youngest of the seven children. Not that Veronica spent all that much time raising them. She was often away on one of her get-rich-quick schemes, so parenting fell to her sister, Edward's Aunt Beatrice. Never married, Beatrice became the nanny who doted on the children. She had saved Edward's life when he was a toddler by forcing milk down his throat after he had swallowed poison. He had tears in his eyes when he talked about Beatrice and said that he hadn't realized the important part she played in his life until years after her death.

Despite Veronica's benign neglect of her children, she was passionate about Leslie. As her husband lay dying, she devoted herself to his care, even as she was forced to transfer him to Nashville's Protestant Hospital, where he became a charity patient in a crowded ward.

"I spoke often with him on the phone," Edward told me. "I heard his confusion. They weren't about to tell him the truth, that he was dying." But Edward kept putting off the trip to Nashville to see his ailing father. When it became clear that Leslie's death was imminent, though, Edward bundled his wife and daughters into their secondhand Chevy sedan. He reasoned that it would take three days to make the trip from Long Island to Nashville, if the car didn't break down along the way. At that time, the superhighways hadn't yet been completed. You could drive on five-to-ten-mile stretches of paved road and then you were back on the old system for fifty to sixty miles at a time. They took the Skyline Drive along the crest of the Blue Ridge Mountains so that the girls could enjoy the dramatic scenery.

"I wanted them to see the cotton candy clouds," said Edward.

It was part of the same route that Paula and Edward took when they made their trip to California as newlyweds. They even stayed at the same tourist home they had stopped at on their wedding night, when they still dreamed that they could make it big in Hollywood. This time Edward was thirty-five, and as he set off on his journey South to see his dying father, his dreams of becoming an actor had long vanished. After he and Paula moved to

California, in the early 1940s, the closest Edward got to Hollywood glamour was filling grocery orders for some of the biggest movie stars of the day at the May Co. in Los Angeles. During the day, he worked as a clerk, taking phone orders from the butlers of Orson Welles, Judy Garland, and Katharine Hepburn, filling their boxes with produce and studying his lines for the amateur theatrical productions he starred in at night. Later, he took a night school course in welding and worked the graveyard shift at the San Pedro shipyard.

In 1941, he landed the lead role in a play called *American Sampler.* One night, a talent scout connected with Columbia Pictures saw one of his performances and asked him to set up a screen test. But Edward's timing was off. His screen test was cancelled after the Japanese attack on Pearl Harbor plunged America into the Second World War.

Weeks later, Edward was called up for military service. He was twenty-three years old, over six feet tall, and barely 130 pounds. After hours of standing in line with dozens of draftees at a federal recruitment office in Los Angeles, waiting for an army doctor to do a physical examination, he collapsed. The room full of men was stuffy, and the next thing he knew he was lying on the floor, while an orderly tried to revive him with smelling salts. Edward had fainted and would soon fail his medical exam.

Four years into their Hollywood sojourn, Edward and Paula made the decision to return to New York for good. His agent suggested that he would have a better chance of being discovered on Broadway by talent agents than in the low-budget theatrical productions he was doing in Hollywood. "Let them find you there," said the agent.

Back in New York, though, acting opportunities dried up. Paula had long since abandoned acting, and now Edward, too, put his performance dreams aside when Paula became pregnant with Laura. They moved into a second-floor walk-up on Jones Street in the Village, but with a baby on the way, they no longer felt comfortable living in cramped quarters in Manhattan. They relocated to the Long Island suburbs, and by the time Valerie arrived seven years later, Edward was working alternately as a tailor and a welder. Later, he sewed upholstery in a car factory.

But Paula and Edward wrote stage plays together at

night. Edward showed me the correspondence they received from one of the biggest producers on Broadway in the 1950s. He wanted to put on one of Edward and Paula's plays, but in the end decided against going with two unknowns. "I was, in 1955, accepting finally that we were not good enough as playwrights," Edward said. "So be it. The girls were growing and I was providing for us essentially, though I should have been earning more to make our lives easier."

Occasionally, to make up the shortfall, Edward took the train to Belmont to bet on the horses. Sometimes he won several thousand dollars. But these events were few and far between.

As he drove across the country on his grim mission to Nashville, a sense of failure overtook him.

"I was headstrong and had more insecurities than Paula should have had to put up with," he confessed to me. "But she didn't push me and was marvelously supportive as well as endlessly appreciative and admiring of me. Well, she loved me, like no one ever could. I was luckier than I had a right to be. I'm ashamed I didn't know it then."

And as he approached his family home in Nashville, he braced himself for what he knew would be a final meeting with his father. But nothing could have prepared him for what he was about to encounter in the hospital room.

"He looked, lying on that bed, like the victims we had seen in Shoah," recalled Edward. The horrors of the Nazi Holocaust had been revealed only a decade earlier. Edward wanted to take his father off life support, to end his suffering, and tried to rally his mother, brothers, and sisters to the cause.

"Fuck the hospital," he had said to his family; this was no way for any human being to die. "He was all protruding blue veins and tubes and wires," recalled Edward. "Tubes from plastic bags overhead fed solutions drop by drop into his veins on quivering arms and body. And from his bladder and colon, contents flowed through more tubes into pans beneath the bed. I begged the intern to remove the tubes and allow him to die with dignity, but no one listened."

That night, as Paula and the children were asleep in his old bedroom, Edward was restless, anxious about his father's suffering. The air was heavy as before a storm, and the city was dark and silent. Edward stared out the second-floor window of his childhood home, straining to catch the intermittent glow of fireflies.

And then he heard chirping and looked out as a lone mockingbird fluttered up and down on a pole in his backyard. Losing himself in the birdsong, Edward felt something graze his leg.

A mouse? A rat?

"I felt that rats were invading the walls of our home, the way the cancer had invaded my father's veins," Edward said. The next day, before heading to the hospital, Edward bought traps and set them up inside the house and in the bushes next to the foundation, right under his father's bedroom window. He was standing in the living room when he heard one of the traps snap shut. At the same time, he became vaguely aware of the doorbell ringing. He ignored the doorbell and rushed to dispose of the trapped rodent. But as he approached the trap, Edward recoiled.

"I saw that I had trapped something gray," said Edward, who began to tear at the memory. "But it wasn't a rat." By now he was sobbing as he struggled to tell me the rest of the story. Before he even managed to get the words out, I knew what he was going to say.

"I killed the mockingbird," he said in a hoarse whisper.

He sat on the ground in the garden of his childhood home cradling the dead bird, a symbol of the South, his youth, and perhaps his innocence. He didn't need to hear the news from the hospital messenger who had been incessantly ringing the doorbell. He already knew that his father was dead.

"I buried the bird, trap and all, in the backyard," said Edward, still crying. "It was the Fourth of July."

The funeral was two days later, and the day after that Edward and his family got in their Chevy to return to New York. Back on the Skyline Drive, Edward was so tired and distraught that he swerved off the highway, "only stopping by some miracle when I slammed my foot on the brake before we would have catapulted off the side down to our deaths below."

We were quiet for what seemed to be a long time after Edward finished his story—until Edward rose from the table and busied himself with the Turkish coffee that he made in a makeshift ibrik on the stove. He poured the thick dark liquid from his coffee pot into two espresso cups and added a few drops of Ricard to each cup.

We drank our little cups of coffee quietly, watching as the fine grains made swirling patterns on the sides of the white cups after each sip, and then collected in a muddy sludge at the bottom by the time we'd finished. What could those grounds tell us about where we were going, where we had come from, and how we ended up here in this hushed dining room in New York City?

Finally, Edward turned to me, smiling. "That's a hell-uva way to end an evening," he said.

13

Linguine with Homemade Pesto
Salad
Assorted Chocolates
Martini, Pinot Grigio

I told Edward I was through with men.

I stood beside him as he warmed plates in the oven and wondered what we were having for dinner. Edward didn't say anything. He didn't even glance my way; he simply had no reaction to my pronouncement. Instead, he opened the freezer, removed a frosty martini glass and the Pyrex cup that contained his magical icy mixture, and poured it into the cold glass. He poured himself one as well.

In the past, whenever I had let him know that I had met an interesting man, Edward seized on the news.

"Bring him over," said Edward, after I mentioned the businessman whose Midwest accent and air of studied earnestness reminded me of Nick Carraway in *The Great Gatsby*.

"I want him to know that you are not alone in the world, that you have someone who is watching over you," he said.

I was deeply touched that Edward had become my protector. But it was also clear that he didn't think much of my ability to take care of myself or make sound judgments—not when it came to men, anyway. Although he claimed that it wasn't me he was worried about. "It's just that I know men, I know how they think, and that's why I worry," he said.

Why was he worried? I never found out. Was it a fatherly concern that any man I met was simply going to use me, and then dump me? Would I become pregnant, and abandoned, like one of his sisters, whose ill-fated affair with her university professor left her a struggling single mother in the 1930s?

The night I announced that I was through with men, I was a bit disappointed that Edward didn't even look up from his stove but continued with the final preparations for our dinner. By now I knew that he was inured to my dramatic declarations, but this silence was still uncomfortable. I was glad when we sat down to our steaming plates of linguine with Edward's pesto.

Maybe Edward was right to be concerned, because when I moved off Roosevelt Island and started to date, I did everything wrong. For one thing, I became determined to find a younger version of Edward, and though I saw glimpses of him in the handful of the men I met, in some dark recess of my brain I must have known this was a recipe for disaster, that I was setting up unrealistic expectations, but I did it anyway.

There was the carpenter who had Edward's soft blue eyes. Like Edward, he had made all of his own furniture; he wrote poetry and he cooked. He'd kissed my hand after he'd walked me home along an icy stretch of road.

There was the SoHo chef with the wild, white hair, the leather jacket, and the moped, who wanted to whisk me to the far reaches of New Jersey for steamed clams and roasted corn on the cob.

I thought I was making a wise choice in the financier. We weren't officially dating. Between his international business trips we'd meet at the Grand Central Oyster Bar.

He spoke passionately about global problems, political corruption, ending human trafficking. He was handsome in an intellectual and absentminded kind of way. He subscribed to the *New York Review of Books*.

My illusions came crashing down when I walked in on him and a woman at a tony Upper East Side restaurant. I later found out she was his wife. I was standing at the espresso bar, hopelessly underdressed in worn Birkenstocks and shorts, as he walked by on his way out. In a linen suit and wraparound sunglasses, his phone plastered to his ear, he looked very different from the smart do-gooder I knew.

"What's wrong with you?" asked my friend, the fashion editor, dressed in black. We had walked into the Madison Avenue eatery so that she could buy a tuna sandwich. "Are you sick? You just went totally pale."

"Don't move," I said. "He's here. With a *woman*."

The fashion editor's face lit up.

"Where?"

I gestured feebly and turned quickly to face the espresso bar, just as he walked behind me, accompanied by a lithe blond wearing tight white jeans and her own aviator sunglasses. I couldn't see much more with my hand holding up my forehead, my elbows on the bar, my gaze fixed on the espresso machine in front of me

He didn't see me. How could he see anything through those wraparound glasses and the aura of self-importance that was as finely tailored as the expensive suit he wore? Strange that I had never noticed it before. But in the split second that I caught him making his way through the crowded restaurant with the leggy woman and a studied nonchalance, he suddenly seemed like a cliché.

The fashion editor craned her neck to have a good look, and then suggested we do the polite and proper thing, which was to say hello. He was out on the sidewalk.

"C'mon, let's go bust him now," she said with obvious glee. "His reaction will tell us everything."

I grabbed her arm.

"I've never seen you this frightened," she said. "Stop it. Let's just go say hello."

"No, we're not leaving the restaurant," I whispered, terror-stricken. "We're standing here and having an espresso."

She gave me a look that combined pity and incomprehension. I tried to explain it in a way that she could best relate to—I pointed to my shorts and yellow Birkenstocks.

"But you look cute," she said.

"I don't want to look cute!"

If you are going to confront the object of your desire who is with another woman, you had better look glamorous and sexy to show him what he is missing.

"OK, I get it, but calm yourself down," said my friend, craning her neck to get a better look at the financier who was still outside the restaurant, still talking on his phone.

The barista made me a perfect espresso in a white and peach porcelain cup. I downed it in one gulp. It was worth $5.

It wasn't like I hadn't been warned. Melissa and I had done our own research in the newsroom, finding a woman's cell phone registered to his name and address. At the *Post*, whenever anyone—mostly one of the twenty-something women reporters—was interested in a man, we would immediately plug his name into every public records database we could access. An e-Courts or Scroll New York search would reveal if he were going through a divorce in the state of New York; a Nexis search would show if he lived with anyone or had any judgments against him; New York's department of finance would let us know if he had any tax liens against him. We could also look up any homes or mortgages, weapons' permits, and criminal records.

In my case, a simple Google image search revealed dozens of photos of the financier and the lithe, blond young woman in back issues of the *New York Social Diary*, the society newsletter for the boldface crowd. I rationalized. Perhaps they had already broken up? Why else would he be texting me, making plans to meet? I was too embarrassed to tell Edward the whole sorry tale. Yes, Edward had cause to worry. I harbored some pretty naïve views about men and love. In a fit of wounded vanity, after the disappointment of the businessman, I decided it was best to give up.

After we had finished our salads and moved on to the box of expensive chocolates that had been given to Edward by one of his neighbors, I told Edward again that I was through with falling in love, that I couldn't imagine at middle age finding the man of my dreams. This time he answered.

"How about a woman?" said Edward, looking up at me, a mixture of incredulity and compassion in his gaze.

14

Crab Cakes with Homemade Tartar Sauce
Tomato Salad with Homemade Pesto Dressing
Prune Tart
Pinot Grigio

We never made it to dessert the night Edward collapsed.

Of course, there was a dessert—there was always dessert chez Edward. On this particular evening it was a prune tart that I glimpsed on the kitchen counter, still steaming from the oven, the prunes oozing their dark syrup onto the golden French pastry. We had just finished our salads, after the crab cakes, and anticipating our next course, Edward began to explain how he had prepared the tart. The secret, he said, was soaking the prunes in Earl Grey tea for at least an hour before baking.

"That's how you get that thick, sweet black syrup," he explained. "Just soak them for an hour before you—"

But he began to tremble and his words came out in a slur before he could take me through the rest of the recipe. And then Edward lurched forward in his straight-back chair. I rushed to help him, and he seemed to will himself back to an upright position. Closing his eyes, with great effort, he steadied himself and slowly rose from his chair, leaning on his cane, which he always kept nearby. He headed to the bathroom, leaving me in his empty living room, wondering if he was ever going to be all right again.

It seemed like a long time that he was gone. I called to him, to ask if he was OK, and he said he would be back momentarily.

I wasn't prepared for what I saw when he limped back into the kitchen, where I was now filling the sink with soapy water. He stood, leaning on his cane, in bare feet, wearing a threadbare nightshirt. A cluster of blue veins balled at his elbows, below a thin layer of almost translucent skin, dotted by liver spots.

Where was *my* Edward, the proud, jovial, and smartly dressed gentleman who had made me an almond cake for my birthday and taken me to Saks Fifth Avenue? Could he really be this frail, elderly man who stood helplessly, his age so harshly revealed under the fluorescent lights of the kitchen? I wanted to look away, suddenly overwhelmed by a wave of embarrassment. I was never supposed to see him like this.

"Don't tell Valerie," he said in what seemed to me a desperate whisper. "And don't tell Laura."

It was the only time I ever betrayed him. It did cross my mind that he might never speak to me again when he found out that I had told his daughters about his near fainting episode. That night, as I walked toward the tram, I called Laura, who rushed over from her apartment across the street to make sure her father was all right. And then I called Valerie.

For months after that, I spoke to Edward only briefly, even after he actually did faint some weeks later. He hurt himself so badly when he fell on the tile floor of his bathroom that he couldn't get out of bed for weeks. He developed bedsores and began fighting with his daughters.

No, he would not go to the hospital. No, he didn't

want to see his doctor; Edward already knew what was ailing him, and he claimed he knew better how to heal himself. Clearly, he was afraid. Did his mind race back to the summer of 1955, when his father lay dying in a Nashville hospital ward "coiled in a fetal position, knees drawn up to his chest, little left but skin, covering protruding bones"?

"Fuck the hospital," he had said then about his father.

Or was he remembering when Paula got sick? One day, Paula took the Roosevelt Island tram into Manhattan and came home more exhausted than usual. It was the last time she would go into the city on her own. "She told me that she was no longer the gal she used to be," said Edward. He paused, thinking about the day that signaled the beginning of the end. "For me, she was always the same," he said, as if trying to convince himself. "She hadn't changed."

But when they went to visit their doctor, there was sobering news. Paula would have to have her leg amputated. The doctor's speech made sense; he even sounded encouraging. "The prosthetics today are phenomenal. She will learn to walk again. She could live another four or five years," he said with enthusiasm.

“No way,” Edward had told the doctor, when they were alone.

If we don’t amputate, the doctor warned him, gangrene could develop: “She’ll have to go to a hospice where they will zonk her out with morphine until the end. However long that might take. Maybe weeks. Not a happy ending.”

But Edward was unmoved. He knew that Paula’s “Appointment in Samarra” was imminent. It was his favorite tale from the Arabian Nights, adapted by Somerset Maugham. He had often told me the story about the Baghdad servant who was sent out to the market to buy provisions for his master, a wealthy merchant. The servant bumped into Death at the market. Frightened, he borrowed his master’s horse and galloped to Samarra to escape his fate. Later, the merchant went to the market to confront Death himself. “Why did you make a threatening gesture to my servant when you saw him this morning?” he asked.

Death looked amused. “That was not a threatening gesture,” said Death. “It was only a start of surprise. I was astonished to see him in Baghdad, for I had an appointment with him tonight in Samarra.”

Edward had told the story about the impossibility of escaping death to another doctor years earlier, when he'd had a brush with cancer. "After an operation, I was advised of a procedure that I was reluctant to take. Chemotherapy is poison. Not vitamins or orange juice," he had written in a fictionalized version of the episode he called "Providence."

Edward recited the Arabian tale to the oncologist who would be administering the therapy, asking "if in relation to that slave seeking escape from Death's beckoning, was I, too, by taking chemo, rushing to my death and Samarra?" The oncologist told him he didn't know. Which is when Edward decided not to proceed. Ten years later, the cancer had still not returned.

But the folktale seemed lost on most medical professionals. "She's a vibrant woman," insisted Paula's doctor in his Upper East Side office. "Why would you want to deny yourselves all the life she has left? You talk it over. She may surprise you. Tell me what you decide."

Paula, though, agreed with Edward. It was a quiet afternoon in August—that time in Manhattan when only sweating tourists clutching maps seem to walk the streets. Edward said little to his wife in the taxi back home. He held her frail hand in his as the cab rattled through sun-baked streets en route to the Queensboro Bridge. Then, desperate, he proposed that they commit suicide together; Paula squeezed his hand, and said that he was being ridiculous; she would have none of it.

Edward took Paula home, where she died two months later, surrounded by their scrapbooks, the rugs she had hooked, the dining room table he had fashioned from scraps of wood that he had found at one of his job sites, the walnut coffee table, the straight-back chairs that he had woven from fine strands of wood, the pillows she had quilted from the remnants of old skirts, fraying cotton sheets, and tartan work shirts that were all testament of their sixty-nine years together.

And now, after his fall, Edward told his daughters, if it was indeed time for his own appointment with death, he was determined to do it surrounded by the things he loved. How would he ever feel better in an anonymous hospital room? He needed to stay where he could glance out the windows and watch the tugboats streaming across the East River during the day and the lights of the million-dollar apartment buildings on the Upper East Side that twinkled at nightfall. What had Paula said about those places when they first moved to their apartment? "They paid millions for their places with their river views, and they are really just looking at us. We paid a fraction of the price, and we have the million-dollar view of Manhattan! How about that?"

Although he had never articulated it until now, he was adamant that, like Paula, he would die at home, without any special care. And so, he resisted his well-meaning daughters at every turn.

Fuck the hospital.

My own father had said much the same when my mother lay in a coma in a hospital room in Toronto. A diabetic, she had suffered a stroke days earlier. Like Edward and Paula, my parents had been married a long time, nearly sixty years. Unlike Edward and Paula, they were extremely reserved. They rarely kissed, almost never exchanged gifts. There were never any vocal declarations of undying love between them, no cards or letters painstakingly collected in a scrapbook. As a kid and then as a young adult, I railed against what I saw as their lack of affection. Hadn't I told each of my husbands how much I loved him?

Now I realize how immature I had been about my

parents. I came to understand how much they had loved each other: In the year before my mother died, my father, a gruff and curmudgeonly seventy-nine-year-old, became her most devoted nurse, administering her insulin five times a day, pricking her finger to draw the drop of blood, placing it on a plastic test strip, which he attached to the glucose meter to measure her blood sugar level. He meticulously recorded each alteration, however slight, in his precise handwriting on a graph that he had designed himself. My father was a carpenter, a construction foreman who had barely managed to complete high school and who had immigrated to Canada with little more than his bag of tools in the early 1950s. But the graph that he showed to my mother's doctors was so detailed that they couldn't believe that it hadn't been put together by a trained medical professional.

My father cried when my mother died. I know this because it was reported to me by someone who saw him do it, discreetly, in her hospital room as an orderly took her body away. I have never seen my father cry. After her funeral, he visited my mother's grave every day in the grand park-like cemetery, which is also the final resting place of Canada's heads of government and captains of industry. My mom's grave is across the way from the crypt belonging to the Massey family, one of the country's most important and wealthiest dynasties, and down the street from William Lyon Mackenzie King, Canada's longest serving prime minister.

It had long been my father's ambition that they should be buried together in this beautiful cemetery—two Portuguese immigrants who felt they had made their own important contributions to their new land, even though they had held no elected office or important titles. Their greatness, according to my father, was that they had embraced their adopted country, worked hard, and loved their two children and four grandchildren. My mother's name, dates of birth and death, are engraved on her black granite headstone, and my father's name and date of birth is carved underneath hers, followed by a hyphen, standing sentinel, awaiting the date of my father's "Appointment in Samarra."

My father rarely misses a day at the cemetery. When we talk to him on the phone, he often tells my brother and me that he is off to visit our mother at "the park." Every time I'm in Canada, we head there together. He knows all the groundskeepers by name, as well as the lonely woman who visits the grave of her husband, which lies down the lane from my mom's grave. He brings takeout coffee and a newspaper to read, dozing off in his car parked next to the headstone on summer afternoons. He pulls out weeds around her grave in the spring, shovels the snow around the headstone in winter.

One early morning, I accompanied him to the cemetery and saw him put a handful of raw peanuts on my mother's headstone. He noticed my quizzical look and held an index finger to his lips.

"Shhhhh," he hissed, pointing to the stone.

I didn't understand at first, and then I saw them. A cardinal and then a blue jay and then sparrows fluttered above the scattered peanuts, finally alighting on the black headstone, come to keep my mother company. Later, I gathered the pinecones that had fallen from the trees near the grave and brought them back to New York in my suitcase. I keep them in a basket in my bedroom.

In one of our few conversations during the long months of Edward's illness, I called Edward to tell him the story of my father. It made him happy, but he didn't have the energy to say much. I longed to help him, but there seemed so little I could do. And then one night, when I was having trouble remembering one of his recipes, I called him again.

"Remind me how you made that Grand Marnier soufflé?" I hoped that talking about food might heal him. I started calling more regularly. When he was sleeping, I would leave messages on his answering machine—questions about some culinary dilemma that only he could resolve.

"Edward, I forgot the trick you taught me with the french fries. Could you call me back?"

"What's the name of that restaurant in Chinatown where you get your duck?"

I like to think my culinary quandaries improved his mood at least.

"Your phone call today about my recovery's progress is much appreciated," he wrote to me when he was starting to feel better, "even though its status quo was not what I should have enjoyed relating to you. But at my age there are no quick fixes to equal the speed in which calamity can leave one disabled. But you allowed me, in your excitement about rendezvousing with soufflés soon, to forget if all too briefly my pain."

When he was well enough to cook again, Edward

began to invite me to dinner. But those evenings lacked the same magic. He no longer sang along to Billie Holiday or Ella Fitzgerald. In fact, there was no music in the apartment. He wasn't up for the walks to his butcher and fishmonger across the Roosevelt Island Bridge to Astoria, so we ate whatever was easy. He rarely went into Manhattan. Often, there was no dessert. And when he did serve sweets, they were the over-the-top pastries Laura bought at Maison Kayser on the Upper East Side.

He tried to rally in celebration of his ninety-third birthday. We had planned a big dinner at Balthazar, one of his favorite restaurants in Manhattan, but in the end he said he didn't have the strength to leave the island. So, we stayed in and had a simple meal—linguine with tomato sauce and prune cupcakes for dessert.

"Edward's turning ninety-three? I thought he was already ninety-three," I said to Laura a week before the dinner.

"He tells everyone that he is ninety-three, and when he actually turns ninety-three, he will be telling everyone that he is in his ninety-fourth year," said Laura.

On the eve of a particularly bad nor'easter, Edward called me to cancel our dinner plans. He was worried that

I wouldn't be able to make it to Roosevelt Island during the storm, even though he lived just a quick subway ride away from my midtown office. But later that afternoon, when the storm proved milder than the weather reports had predicted, he called to reschedule. But by the end of the day I received a third phone call at my office. Dinner was indeed cancelled.

Edward apologized profusely for the confusion. "I no longer have control of my life," he confessed to me over the phone in a rare outpouring of fear. "I feel shaky. I'm frightened so easily now. I'm losing control. I'm aware that I'm losing control of my life."

By the third phone call, I became determined to visit him anyway, and see for myself how he was doing. "No need to prepare dinner," I said. "We can just have a drink."

I let myself into the apartment, where I found Laura fussing in the kitchen. Edward had made flounder, and there was acorn squash dusted with brown sugar in the oven. Things seemed to have returned to normal, but when Edward appeared outside his bedroom door dressed in a frayed, white terrycloth robe, he announced that he was going to bed even though it wasn't quite six o'clock. Laura and I would have to amuse ourselves, he said.

Neither of us felt like eating. We sat in the living room for a long time, drinking Scotch. Laura's husband had recently died. They had returned to New York from Greece when he became ill and Laura had nursed him here. Now newly widowed, she frequently dined at her father's apartment. Laura had spent the last several months taking care of Edward and had borne the brunt of his anger and frustration. She cried when she started to speak.

"I just don't want to spend the rest of my life looking after sick people," she said as the tears streamed down her face. "You don't know what it's like until you have to do it."

Laura's husband, only a few years younger than Edward, had been her art teacher in Piraeus, where she went to study as a young, aspiring artist. The walls of Edward's apartment are crowded with Laura's work—chalky pastels of blues and yellows, evoking the idea of the soft lingering afternoon light on the Greek port city where she and her husband had lived for years.

I went home that night feeling low, worried about

Edward, worried about Laura, too. I longed for our dinners à deux.

And then, finally, Edward was feeling better, behaving more like, well, Edward. One night he invited me to dinner. Laura was there as well. As I was preparing to take my leave, Edward escorted me to the elevator. We lingered as he authoritatively lifted his cane to prevent the elevator from descending until he was finished speaking.

"I miss the dinners we used to have—just you and me," he said, as if reading my mind.

That night, I left his apartment feeling relieved, but also as though I had lost something. Edward must have noticed that things were not right because the next morning, before I woke up, I had the following message on my phone: "I just wanted to call and tell you how much I enjoyed you being here last night, your coming, your being here made it very special," he said. "I'm sorry that it wasn't just a dinner between you and me, but we'll have those dinners again sometime in the future, I hope."

And then, as if to convince himself, he added, "We'll have them and enjoy them again. Good night, baby."

15

Canapes of Sun-Dried Tomato and Chèvre
Cream of Cauliflower Soup with
Truffle Oil and Dried, Reconstituted
Porcini Mushrooms
Prime Rib
New Potatoes, Haricots Verts
Grand Marnier Soufflé with Fresh Cream
Turkish Coffee
Cabernet Sauvignon

It was to be a triumphant feast—the dinner Edward would prepare to signal that he was back, and he was going to do it in grand style.

He took the bus to his Queens butcher to pick up the prime rib he had ordered the week before and was absorbed with the preparations for a dinner that was to include neighbors and friends who had seen him through his long illness. He would invite the aging Czech artist and his beautiful wife, the Albanian refugee couple who had fled persecution in Montenegro, and the dentist and his wife. Laura would also be there and, as usual, he asked me to be his sous chef.

I was looking forward to seeing Edward in his element again, but a few days before the big event, I was rearranging the furniture in my apartment and pushed one of my bulky bookcases. I didn't think much of the slight pain I felt in my back. The next day, though, I could barely get out of bed. The pain was so excruciating that putting on a pair of socks became a twenty-minute ordeal. At the doctor's office I couldn't even sit in the waiting room, so I stood rigidly against a counter at reception, barely able to support myself upright until a nurse came out to fetch me.

The pain was particularly intense when I sneezed or coughed. Laughing was also unbearable, and I stayed in bed in various positions of discomfort. After several days of swallowing painkillers and affixing sticky pain patches to the inflamed spot on my back, I was feeling only slightly better. I called Edward to tell him the bad news: I was going to miss his big comeback dinner.

"I'm so sorry you won't be able to make it, darling," he said.

I asked him what he was cooking.

Prime rib with steamed haricots verts and potatoes au jus would be the spectacular main course. He was also serving martinis and goat cheese canapés with sun-dried tomatoes before the meal and a sublime Grand Marnier soufflé with hints of orange zest and topped with fresh cream for dessert. But Edward was particularly excited about the soup course he was planning.

"I was so looking forward to having you try my cauliflower soup," he told me on the phone.

Cauliflower soup?

"Yes, with truffle oil and reconstituted dried mushrooms."

The idea of cauliflower soup with truffle oil sounded simply too delicious and I asked Edward to give me the recipe right there and then.

"Well, first, you sweat the onions. You add some good chicken stock, and then you stir in the cauliflower pieces," he said by way of explanation. "You cook them down, and then you use an inversion blender to mix everything together." The truffle oil and the reconstituted mushrooms are added as garnishes at the end, he said.

I don't know why I felt compelled to make that soup,

but after I wrote down Edward's instructions, I put on my clothes with great difficulty, popped a few painkillers, and headed to the nearest Fairway to buy the ingredients. I spent an inordinate amount of time weighing the differences between white and black truffle oil. I knew nothing about truffle oil, so I finally opted for the black—an unfortunate choice I learned back home when I called Edward.

"What were you thinking, kid?" he asked, both incredulous and amused that I would make such an egregious error in culinary judgment. He prefers the white, which he says is stronger and mustier than the black and has less of a garlicky flavor. Edward and I had unwittingly landed in the middle of a flap that had been heating up among some of the world's greatest chefs about the legitimacy of truffle oil. Most truffle oils are nothing more than a chemical compound, comprised of olive oil and "flavoring." Edward checked the label of his bottle, which denoted that it had been made with infused truffles. He had the good stuff. I peered at the label on my bottle. Mine was indeed the fake. A wave of anger swept over me as I read, "olive oil, flavoring." So now my wrong-color oil wasn't even the real thing.

I was in too much pain to return to Fairway but still determined to make the soup. I spent the evening cutting up onions and cauliflower and slowly cooking the mixture. Like Edward, I now had to grip the counters when I moved. I stood carefully on the step stool I used to fish ingredients and cooking implements out of cupboards that were beyond my reach. I puréed the cooked cauliflower and onions in the blender and the result was a velvety potage. I soaked dried porcini mushrooms, chopped them, and lightly fried them in olive oil.

I ladled out the soup, topped it with the mushrooms, swirled my fake black truffle oil over the top, and served bowls of soup to my daughter and her friend. I stood at the kitchen counter to eat. Maybe it was the medication finally kicking in, but as we ate I felt no pain. The soup, with the musky richness of the truffle oil and the porcini, made me feel better immediately.

"The inspiration can kill a lot of troubles," Rita once said when we were talking about making some of Edward's specialties. For Rita, it was Edward's soufflé that took her through some of the rough periods in her life. For me, it became the cauliflower soup. I like to think that Edward had a hand in making us all feel better.

Truthfully, after a momentary reprieve from the soup, I was not completely healed. That would take a few more weeks and during that time I became acutely aware that I had no one to count on in a time of crisis. Clearly I could no longer call on my husband to help me move furniture or hang pictures in my apartment. These were small things, to be sure, but shortly after moving to Central Park South I realized I barely knew how to handle a screwdriver. A girlfriend offered to loan me a power drill, but I demurred because I had no idea what to do with it and I didn't want to hurt myself.

Worse, though, there was really no one to help me through my convalescence. Who would apply the Lidocaine patches to my lower back to ease the pain? Who would be there for me in the way that Paula and Edward had taken care of each other, in the way that my father had monitored my mother's blood sugar and administered her insulin? I could barely get myself into a sitting position, let alone do laundry or make a cup of tea. How would I ever be able to walk up and down stairs? Who would support me if I could no longer work?

"I know how limited I am in many activities I once did earlier in my life, easily without thought," Edward had written to me during his own illness. "And it leaves me feeling defenseless."

I was also feeling defenseless, and his words flew through my mind in my worst moments. I thought of Edward who had to face the pain of aging alone. It was all a part of what he liked to call a normal life.

"People are too obsessed with seeking experience and feel that if they are not living on the razor's edge, they are not alive," Edward had once told me. "It's because they can't deal with normal life. They need to climb Mount Everest instead."

I had been one of those people whom Edward was talking about. I had lived on the razor's edge. I had voluntarily traveled to extreme places, to cover war in Africa and drug traffickers in South America. And I thought the experience was more valid than the daily grind. I had always lived with the notion that paradise was somewhere else. But Edward knew better. He knew that paradise was not a place, but the people in your life. How many times had he repeated to me, "Paradise was me and Paula"?

When I was finally feeling better, I called Edward and let him know about the miracle of the soup cure. He wasn't at all surprised. His dinner party had gone off well, he said, and he had missed me. He also told me that we had a special connection because we had come together when we were both vulnerable. When Paula died, he had suddenly felt he was old for the first time in his life.

"When you come for dinners with me, we talk hungrily about those matters and problems we each face," he later wrote in a letter to me.

That night, I sat down to write my own letter to Edward. I told him that I had never been incapacitated like this, and how I was suddenly feeling middle-aged and alone. I told him that he had saved my life and that he would be with me forever.

The response was swift. Edward called me right after he read my letter.

"You saved your own life," he said. "You think about this in time and you will come to see the truth of what I'm saying. You were giving as well as receiving." And then his voice caught, and he said he needed to go. "You touched an old man's heart."

16

Chicken Liver Pâté, Crackers
Flounder alla Francese over Steamed Spinach
Grilled Sweet Potatoes
Chocolate Cake
Riesling

Edward and Paula's wedding anniversary was in early November. To celebrate Edward invited me to dinner.

It was just the two of us, and we settled into a long-forgotten routine. I presented Edward with a bottle of wine. It was a Portuguese rosé, a wine more appropriate for a summer meal than the pre-winter feast we were about to enjoy. But I knew Edward loved the wine and I couldn't resist bringing him a bottle when I saw it in the store. He promptly labeled it with my name and stored it in his hall closet in the makeshift cellar behind the winter coats.

In the kitchen, he offered me a plate of his homemade chicken liver pâté. The creamy pâté was sublime, with hints of cognac and cream. I spread it on crackers as I watched Edward prepare our meal. He limped to the refrigerator and removed two pieces of flounder, which he had coated in flour, bathed in an egg wash, and rolled in bread crumbs.

The fish fillets sizzled for about three minutes. They sizzled but never smoked because Edward did all of his frying and sautéing with clarified butter. He had a small container of it in his refrigerator and explained to me that he melted butter and waited until it solidified before he removed the watery whey that caused the butter to smoke and burn. Edward removed the pan-fried fish fillets to a platter and wiped the hot skillet clean with a paper towel.

"Put a dab of veg or chicken or beef bouillon in pan and sauté on med heat," he wrote me after I asked how he made the sauce. Then he added vermouth, chopped fresh thyme, and strained the sauce with a fine mesh strainer, returning it to the skillet, adding more stock and finishing it off with a squeeze of lemon juice.

Now, ordering me to step aside, he took warm plates from his oven, filled them with steamed spinach, and perched the steaming flounder covered with the lemony sauce on the green beds.

As we sat down to eat, I wanted to tell him about everything that had happened to me over the last several days, but something stopped me. Would he think me foolish? Immature?

"When did you first tell Paula you loved her?" I asked him.

Edward gave me a quizzical look, but he knew better than to answer my question with a question. I'd teased him too many times about that habit.

"The very first day we were together," he said. "On that first night I told her I loved her." He smiled and gave me a long look. "When you know, you just know," he said, downing the remains of his wine in a single gulp.

Was there something I wanted to tell him? his expression seemed to ask. But how could I possibly describe to Edward the breathless events of the past few weeks? After all, I was still processing everything myself.

When you know, you just know.

I knew the first time I saw him, in his well-appointed office in midtown Manhattan, where I showed up to interview him for an article. He spoke fervently about his work, and all I could do was stare at his hands. They were rough and callused and seemed out of place on the gray-suited attorney with close-cropped salt and pepper hair sitting too upright in the wood-paneled office.

Who is he? I thought.

But there were no clues to his identity. No framed family photographs on his desk, no wedding band on his finger. Only the stack of *Food and Wine* magazines under his desk and a collection of vodka bottles on his shelves offered glimpses into his personality.

He cooks! I thought.

On our first date, we walked nearly half the length of Manhattan holding hands. The good-night kiss outside my apartment building was so passionate the doormen on duty teased me for weeks. I walked into the lobby alone, blushing violently.

The first time he came over to my apartment, he brought me fourteen Ziploc bags of herbs that he had carefully cut, separated, and cleaned. They were from the garden of his home, a ranch-style bungalow he had recently bought on a canal on the east end of Long Island. He proudly showed me photographs of the renovations he had just completed. I made him Edward's shrimp and corn chowder. The herbs reminded me instantly of Edward. And, like Edward, I stored most of them in the freezer.

But it was Hurricane Sandy that really brought us together. For a few days after the storm hit, I felt that I had returned to covering a war. New York was battered by Sandy and for days Manhattan south of Thirtieth Street remained a disaster zone, with no subway service or electricity. Ninety percent of Long Island was in the dark.

In the early hours of the storm, my little corner of Manhattan experienced a heightened state of emergency. And while there were no sandbags outside the Russian Tea Room for this hurricane, the aftermath might have been described as equally strange. On the night Sandy struck, I rushed to cover the story of a crane that dangled precipitously from the seventieth floor of an unfinished residential skyscraper on West Fifty-Seventh Street, right near my apartment. I had seen the crane snap in high winds outside a window in my building and held my breath imagining that it would crash onto the street. Up close, the swaying crane seemed attached by a string to the towering half-finished development, where a penthouse apartment had just sold to a Russian billionaire for $115 million.

Flashing my press credentials, I tried to sneak through the yellow tape that the New York City Fire Department had used to cordon off the street. But I didn't make it beyond the back entrance of the New York Athletic Club two blocks away. Two cops told me to stay put, and I found myself packed into a crowd of exasperated New Yorkers who sat with their beautifully groomed dogs and overnight bags. They had been evacuated from their tony apartment buildings situated directly underneath the crane. Many of the upscale refugees had already gone to the second-floor bar for a drink. The ones who were hanging out in the lobby were not allowed to go upstairs because of the club's strict rules governing pets. The elderly man, dressed in tweeds and a raincoat, who wearily slid into the seat beside me, said he was homeless now that he had been forced out of his building. It was but a momentary state of affairs, though. A few minutes later his wife got off the phone with the Harvard Club, where they were members. She secured them a room at $400 a night.

Edward laughed when I told him this story over chocolate cake. I could not yet find a way to tell him what happened a few days later: I waited on East Fortieth and Third Avenue for the Hampton Jitney—the bus that makes regular stops in the villages and hamlets that dot the north and south forks of Long Island. I was headed toward the coast, the storm-ravaged danger zone, to the outer reaches of Long Island, where hundreds of homes had been destroyed, where tens of thousands were without electricity, and where there were long lineups at all the gas stations the jitney passed on the Long Island Expressway. I had packed essentials—rubber boots, food, wine. On the bus, I cursed when I realized that I had forgotten a flashlight, a Swiss Army knife.

All I knew was that the attorney refused to evacuate his home during the worst of the storm. Later, he showed me where he had sat out the tempest alone, facing the living room window in his rocking chair, surveying the rushing floodwaters as they came to within three feet of the house he had moved into just a few months before. To this day, that's the image that always comes to mind when I think of him—a modern-day cowboy defending the homestead.

The night I arrived, we rode bicycles along darkened streets, where the ravages of the storm were everywhere—roadways blocked by felled tree branches, downed power lines, and the occasional frightened deer. The ostentatious summer homes near the shore were shuttered and eerily empty, and the sky was streaked an inky gray and black.

When I moved to New York, I had dreamed of the landscape on the eastern end of Long Island that I'd seen only in photographs, imagined visiting the strips of land that jutted out into the Atlantic Ocean. Sagaponack, Shinnecock, Quogue, Montauk—the names were elemental, pure, ancient, like F. Scott Fitzgerald's "fresh, green breast of the new world." At the end of *The Great Gatsby*, Fitzgerald describes the view that greeted seventeenth-century Dutch sailors when they came upon the coast of Long Island. "For a transitory enchanted moment man must have held his breath in the presence of this continent, compelled into an aesthetic contemplation he neither understood nor desired, face to face for the last time in history with something commensurate to his capacity for wonder."

The wind was calm as we walked hand in hand along the deserted beach. I felt Fitzgerald's "transitory enchanted moment" and I held my breath in the presence of this landscape and this extraordinary man.

"There is somewhere someone who will feel lucky knowing you. And if lucky enough, loving you." The words from one of Edward's early letters—a message so crucial that he had walked to my apartment building on Roosevelt Island over dangerously slippery, ice-packed sidewalks to deliver it to my doorman. Now his lines came back to me in a flood of emotion. But I recognized that I was the lucky one.

That night, after the storm, on that dark beach, he held my hand and whispered, "Thank you for rescuing me." And I couldn't stop smiling. For, really, it was me who had been saved.

17

Grilled Steak
Mashed Potato Croquettes
Sugar Snap Peas Sautéed in Butter
Various Pastries
Lemon-Infused Gin Martini
Merlot

I could tell Edward was grilling steak even before I entered his apartment. The front door was slightly ajar, and when I walked in a cold blast of air blew my hair back. He had left most of the windows open to circulate air in the apartment.

I had returned to Roosevelt Island on assignment and had spent the day staking out a government bureaucrat outside her Main Street office, just a block or so from Edward's apartment building. We had received a tip that the bureaucrat was using a state car at government expense to drive from her home in Westchester to Roosevelt Island, and that state employees were spending their work time walking the bureaucrat's dog. It wasn't exactly Watergate, but it was the kind of waste of government money that the *Post* loves to expose. By now I was a pro at these.

Since I left the island a couple of years ago, I had rarely returned in daylight and so hadn't observed all the changes that had taken place. The southern part of the island was cordoned off as construction crews tore down some of the old hospital complexes to make way for Cornell University's new campus. Edward's building had become a pricey co-op. After the building's board voted to privatize the complex, apartments started to sell for market value. Edward was shocked when he learned that his one-bedroom could now fetch nearly one million dollars. Not that he was planning to sell. I knew he was determined to stay in his apartment until he died.

New shops had started opening on Main Street, including a liquor store, a nail salon, and an organic grocery store. I installed myself at the nail salon and paid an exorbitant price for a manicure/pedicure so that I could sit at their window, which afforded a clear view of the government office I was staking out.

As my nails dried, I sipped the remains of a cold coffee and watched life unfold on the street: Children waiting for school buses crowded the sidewalks and residents headed toward the East River promenade clad in upscale jogging clothes. In fact, life seemed so pleasant that the photographer who later joined me on assignment was thoroughly impressed: "Wow, I never imagined it could be so nice here."

I said nothing. The island was still a difficult place for me because of the memories of my separation and the sensation of being incarcerated at my old apartment complex, The Octagon. Whenever I came back it was mostly under the cover of night, when I was invited to Edward's.

Today he was expecting me for an unusually early dinner and had already started cooking by the time I knocked on the open door. I shivered as I took off my coat. When Edward grills steak or lamb, he uses a cast-iron skillet that he says needs to be scorching hot. And because New York City apartments tend to have only rudimentary ventilation, the resultant smoke sends his fire alarm into beeping panic mode. A brisk wind blew into the apartment from the open windows, and I longed for him to start the steaks so that they would finish and we could shut out the cold.

But Edward was in no hurry. He had marinated flank steaks in balsamic vinegar and taken the meat out of the refrigerator "to allow it to rest" before he began grilling. Now Edward was making us martinis in the kitchen. He had placed two martini glasses in the freezer and was in the process of zesting a lemon. He added the lemon zest to the cup of gin that he had also chilled and, after about ten minutes, filtered the lemony gin before he added dry vermouth. He returned the mixture to the freezer for a few minutes, and finally he poured the cocktails into the chilled glasses with a flourish. We toasted to Paula's memory before Edward tasted his creation.

"This is the best martini I've ever had in my whole life," said Edward, with a sense of triumph that I had never seen before.

"Really?"

But Edward had turned his back and was occupied with the steaks and with sautéing sugar snap peas. He put his potato croquettes in the oven and set everything out on his pre-warmed white dinner plates.

I took another sip of my martini and then I apologized

to Edward for not calling him on the anniversary of Paula's death. I had promised him I would call and then promptly forgot, even as I stopped by his apartment to borrow a book that I wanted to read. But the truth was even worse. I had actually forgotten the anniversary itself.

Of course, Edward never forgot the significance of October 19th. He never forgot the magical serenade Paula performed before she died, and the promise he had made to her to keep on living after she was gone. "My funny valentine, sweet comic valentine, you make me smile with my heart. . . . you're my favorite work of art."

"She grew weak and needed to sleep, saying she would sing more but first, 'just a little nap,' and closed her eyes for the last time," wrote Edward, in a cream-colored leporello—the tribute card he made in honor of Paula. He gave me a copy of the leporello, sheathed in a protective wax paper envelope, the first time we met. I don't know why I didn't open it until more than a year later. When I moved to Central Park South, I found "About Paula," still in its waxy envelope, untouched among some of the letters Edward had written to me.

I took out the elegant card, which unfolded like an accordion over several pages. There are two portraits of

Paula: one with the familiar outstretched chin and dangly gold earrings, a confident smile; the other is much softer, showing a more contemplative Paula. The rest is a collection of Edward's poetry and prose detailing Paula's illness and her last day on earth. The last passage is an imagined dialogue between Paula and Death. Paula tells Death that she can't die until she knows that Edward will continue living.

"I sat weeping, knowing all she had been thinking about was the need to make me change my mind. I thought about her refusal to die until she had done all she could to accomplish that," wrote Edward. Of course, he did change his mind and he kept that promise to Paula.

Edward repeatedly told me he was an atheist (and I suspect Paula was, too) but every year on the anniversary of Paula's death, he insisted on observing Paula's Jewish heritage. He willed himself to stay up late, and at the stroke of midnight—when October 18th becomes the 19th—Edward lights a yahrzeit candle that burns for a full twenty-four hours.

"I wish he wouldn't leave that candle burning like that," said Laura when I showed up to borrow the book from Edward on the day of the anniversary.

I looked at the candle and then glanced at Laura in confusion.

"My mother's death," she said simply. I could hear the fear and frustration in her voice that her elderly father had gone to take a nap and left the candle burning on his cluttered desk. She must have arrived right before me.

The apartment was in a bit of disarray. There were paintings that Edward had removed from the living room walls, ghostly rectangles of the faded paint marking where they used to hang. There were pots spread out on old newspapers on the kitchen counter. Edward must have been in the midst of polishing them. Some of the pots still had the powdery streaks of the copper solution he used in his periodic cleaning of his kitchen tools. He always polished the pots until their copper bottoms gleamed.

I went to the living room shelves and found the book I needed to borrow—*The Force of Things: A Marriage in War and Peace*—a memoir of an extraordinary marriage. I had given the book to Edward for his birthday, and he raved about it so much that I asked to borrow it. The book, by *New Yorker* writer Alexander Stille, details the tempestuous forty-year marriage of his parents, two New Yorkers—a Russian-Jewish journalist who lived in exile in Italy before moving to New York, where he meets his American wife at a party for Truman Capote in 1948. When I read the description of the book and dipped into some of its pages. I couldn't help but think of Edward and Paula, and their very special relationship.

Stille is clear-eyed about his parents' shortcomings and describes some of the epic battles they waged during his childhood, but he also celebrates his parents' intense and enduring bond, told against the backdrop of war and exile. As Stille writes, "Our lives have meaning—above and beyond our individual qualities—because we are part of and express the times in which we live." This resonated with Edward, who read the book in just a few days. He called to tell me how much he loved it, and that he was planning to buy copies to give to his friends.

I told Laura that I probably should write Edward a note telling him that I had borrowed the book. But mostly I wanted to let him know that I had made a point of dropping by on the anniversary of Paula's death, even though my visit was purely accidental and I would have otherwise completely forgotten the date. But Laura promised that she'd tell Edward I was there and I left without leaving him a note.

The year before, near the anniversary of Paula's death, Edward had called me at work to relate a remarkable event. He had awoken shortly after midnight the night before to go to the bathroom, noticed that a light was on in the living room, and was momentarily confused. Was it Valerie, who sometimes stayed up to read when she visited? But Valerie wasn't visiting. Was it Laura? But why would Laura come to him in the middle of the night? Had he left a light on by accident?

No, he said, it was Paula. He had received what he called "a visitation" from Paula, and he wanted to let me know. "I thought you would be happy," he said over the phone.

He was right, of course. And I was happy that he had called to tell me. "You've made my day!" I said. "Thank you, Edward."

I was deeply distressed when I realized that I had missed such an important date. After all, Edward remembered all the significant days in my life—my birthday, my daughter's birthday. He even remembered the day in 2010 that he says I was "reborn." It was easy to remember, coming as it did on Valentine's Day, although it was the antithesis of romantic: It was February 14th when I entered a legal office in midtown Manhattan to sign the sheaf of documents that became my formal petition for divorce.

There may have been a subconscious poetic justice of signing a divorce petition on Valentine's Day but I regret the timing of it now. I'm not sure what's worse, my callous disregard for the day's significance or the complete absence of a romantic soul. I suspect the latter was a far more egregious offense to someone such as Edward. And maybe that's why the date stuck in his mind.

At one point Edward was so ever-present in my thoughts that I easily remembered everything—his birthday, his wedding anniversary, his daughters' birthdays, and even his grandson's birthday. I had first met Andrew as a three-year-old who accompanied his mother, Valerie, to work. They would stop off for bagels across the street from her office in Toronto, and a nanny would take him home or to preschool. Even though Andrew was approaching his thirties, I still kept up with the important milestones in his life through Edward and Valerie.

But now, truth was, I was wrapped up in the euphoria of my blossoming relationship. The pockets of my coats rattled with the green beach glass from our walks on the windswept Hamptons beach. I had little time for my friends; I spoke less to Edward, and that was usually by phone. Every Friday, as soon as I finished with my deadlines, I took off for the Long Island village by the sea that was the scene of my newfound happiness.

My life had changed completely since I first dined with Edward. Now I boarded the Long Island Railroad every weekend, reading books and working at my computer on the lengthy rides through the gritty parts of Queens and through pine forests and the picturesque beach towns that rushed through my window on the Montauk line. Once there, we drove a convertible with the top down even in winter, my hands red and raw from gripping a cold steering wheel, but heady with an exciting sense of freedom.

In the summer I grew herbs, potatoes, onions, garlic, and a handful of vegetables in the garden. I made my own cheese, ice cream, and little jars of jelly from the tiny, bright red crab apples that freighted the branches of an old tree that overlooked the canal behind the bungalow I now shared on the weekends with the man I loved. We watched back-to-back episodes of Julia Child's *The French Chef*, and on our first New Year's

Eve we made her delicate fish mousseline, blending haddock with cream and butter and parsley in the new red Kitchen Aid mixer we had bought the day before. We toasted with champagne and slurped down a tray of oysters before digging into the fluffy mousseline. After that first forkful, we looked up from our plates and smiled at each other—it was surely one of the best things we had ever tasted.

"There is a communion of more than our bodies when bread is broken and wine drunk," wrote M. F. K. Fisher. Eating our mousseline and oysters, a fire roaring in the woodstove in this silent winter seascape, there was also a sense of enchantment, of grace and wonder that we were together and sharing this exquisite meal.

As EDWARD AND I finished our meal, a fall wind whistled outside his fourteenth-floor windows, which we had finally been able to shut. I would be lying if I said that the food that night was superb. The steak was slightly over-cooked, the snap peas mushy because they had sat in the skillet too long. The potatoes were the exception—crispy with a creamy inside. Edward walked to the refrigerator to take out a box of pastries, placing them on a plate—half a chocolate éclair, a pink and white cylinder of what looked like cheesecake decorated with an artfully sliced strawberry. I looked up at Edward, who had already settled on the half-eaten éclair. The cheesecake was mine and was disappointing. It had sat too long in the fridge; it was vaguely reminiscent of ricotta, swirled with sugar and cream. I ate it anyway, accompanied by the rest of my merlot, longing for one of Edward's homemade desserts and wondering if I should bring up the letter I had received from Edward a few days before.

It was dated "Friday 2:38 a.m." and written to finally address the heartfelt letter I had written to him some weeks earlier. Edward's letter said, in part, "The thought you expressed that I am not as understanding of the depth of feeling I have made on you in our friendship leaves me querulous, somewhat sad."

He went on, "It is not easy to appreciate how much strength we expend in establishing and maintaining relationships of varying depths. And when young enough for our bodies to create the energy needed to exist, we take it for granted without analyzing this fact of life. But let me tell you that this age I'm into now is revealing a lot of things I never imagined existed."

Just what had he been trying to say?

For one thing, he told me that he regretted never having told people how much they meant to him when they were alive, in the way I had told him. There were people who had changed Edward's life, who had tremendous meaning to him, but most of them had passed away without ever knowing how he felt about them. There was his aunt Eleanor, who had taken him under her wing when he was a teenager and introduced him to a world of elegance and haute cuisine; his aunt Beatrice, who saved his life when he swallowed the poison, and then practically raised him and his brothers and sisters; his mother, his father, his high-school drama teacher who gave him the envelope with $12 to begin his acting life in the big city; his Manhattan physician who had taken care of him and Paula for decades. And there was Paula, of course, who had completely altered his life.

"I'm sure they knew," I said. "Paula knew."

But Edward was not convinced, and still seemed lost in thought as he walked me to the elevator. Later, he called to thank me for the bottle of the wine I brought him. It was my now customary Portuguese rosé, which he had labeled and put in his hall closet wine cellar. I told him to open it the next time he had someone over for dinner, and not to wait for me.

"I can't wait for anybody anymore," he said plainly.

"What do you mean?" I asked, suddenly alarmed.

He laughed. "Only God knows."

18

The Last Supper

Edward swore me to secrecy about what he jokingly referred to as The Last Supper.

He wanted to throw a big dinner party. He would extend his dining table with the wooden leaf to accommodate all of his guests, who would be a mix of old people he had known for a long time and also new people whom he had never hosted.

This dinner would begin with his guests seated in the living room, where he would serve his lemon-infused gin martinis and savory tartines—thin slices of toasted baguette, topped with his homemade cognac chicken liver pâté.

Then, at the dining room table, he planned to serve small bowls of New England clam chowder, made with heavy cream, potatoes, and fresh Long Island clams from his fishmonger in Astoria. He would slow roast a pork shoulder, slicing it thinly and serving it with baked prunes. He would bake squash, with a hint of brown sugar and dab of cold butter. For dessert, individual apricot soufflés and Turkish coffee. There would be jazz in the background; maybe Ella Fitzgerald or Ute Lemper performing Kurt Weill in her animated German. Maybe even Thelonius Monk.

But while Edward dreamed about preparing dinner, I worried that it had too much of the air of finality about it. Shortly after he turned ninety-four, he had sent a letter to his circle thanking everyone for their birthday wishes. In it, he contemplated his own advanced age.

"When my professed age becomes known, the skepticism I encounter is beginning to become comedic," he wrote. "But if the gods have made some mistake, am I to blame?" He attributed his youthful energy to Paula's enduring love. "The song 'Younger Than Springtime,' was her mantra and being so close I couldn't avoid being touched."

I had also been touched by Edward and Paula's enchanted love story, even though I had never met Paula. To borrow from that Rogers and Hammerstein song she adored so much, during my own dinners with Edward I felt my heart grow strong, and now, years later, I held a world in my embrace. I couldn't allow myself to think that it could all come to an end one day. But, of course, it would.

"Life is not stationary," he continued in his missive. "I'm growing very old in spite of my deceptive appearance."

I didn't want to believe it. And I didn't want this final dinner with Edward, this last supper. After I received his letter, I refused to talk about the dinner or commit to any dates. Then I came up with an idea: I would cook the dinner and Edward would be my guest. It would be the perfect dinner, evidence and appreciation of everything I'd learned from him. I would invite people he knew and people he didn't know.

Edward feigned resistance, but when I dropped by to tell him my idea I could see that he was intrigued.

I had arrived unexpectedly, without an invitation. It

was cocktail hour and Edward busied himself making drinks and filling a bowl with salted cashews. For me, he mixed ice-cold lemony gin and vermouth into a martini glass. Then he poured Canadian whiskey into a tumbler for himself and added some ice. He swirled the amber liquid around in his glass, knocking the ice cubes together before he spoke.

He told me he was grateful that I had come into his life right after he lost Paula, when he needed attention and affection. "And while Laura was still in Greece and Valerie was in Toronto, we formed a bond over dinner. We gave each other the courage to go on with our lives. We were equally giving and receiving in that period, which was crucial to you and me," he said.

Edward had nourished me with more than just food. Yes, he had made magnificent feasts and even plain meals, and I remember each of them still so vividly because every dinner with Edward sustained me "truly against the hungers of the world," as M. F. K. Fisher wrote.

And then he suddenly set his whiskey glass down on the table and grabbed my arm, his twinkling blue-gray eyes welling with tears: "Nobody knows how much we love each other."

"Of course they do, Edward," I said, suddenly overwhelmed.

"No," he insisted. "Nobody knows because I've never told them."

I took a sip of my martini to prevent myself from crying.

I felt that Edward and I had now come full circle and I remembered what I had written in the card I gave him on his birthday. Distracted, I had mailed it to the wrong apartment, but it magically ended up in his mailbox on the day of his birthday. "May you have as many more years as you desire," I wrote. "And know that for me you already live forever."

Now the tears rolled down my cheeks. I grabbed my empty martini glass and walked to the kitchen so that Edward wouldn't notice. I moved some plates around in the sink until I could compose myself, and then I walked back into the living room, where Edward sat finishing his drink, staring out at the shimmering lights of Manhattan and wiping away his own tears with a cocktail napkin.

"So you'll come to my dinner, Edward?" I asked, my voice cracking despite my best efforts to keep it together.

He smiled. And did I detect the slightest nod of agreement?

"Just don't give away my secret on the martini, baby," he said.

Never!

I clasped his hand and we walked toward the elevator. As usual, he held the door open with his cane. He was about to say something. Perhaps he wanted to tell me where to buy the best Turkish coffee, where to get the freshest clams for the chowder, or not to forget to brine the pork in apple cider. Two days, for best results, he always said. Or maybe there was a last bit of wisdom he wanted to impart.

But I was having none of it. I had a lot to do before our next dinner.

"Seven o'clock," I said. "I'll be expecting you."

After-Dinner Talk

An Interview with Isabel Vincent

Edward died just as the hardcover edition of Dinner with Edward *was published. Did he have a chance to read the book?*

Yes, Edward read the book and he was very grateful that I had taken the time to write it. He cried when I first showed him the manuscript. But once he started reading it, he said, "Why would anyone care about my life? I'm not a celebrity." But that's precisely why I think people care—Edward was an ordinary extraordinary person! I also think he was being slightly coy because he had told me that he had filled many scrapbooks throughout his life and worried about what would happen to them after he died. I took this as my cue to write a book about him.

And what about Edward's daughters? What were their reactions?

I think there was some element of shock. Imagine seeing your own life and your father's life told by someone else. It's jarring. But they both told me they read the whole manuscript in one sitting and they are two of the book's biggest supporters. In fact, Edward's memorial at the art gallery on Roosevelt Island doubled as a kind of book launch. Many of those who attended were Edward's neighbors, each of whom had a story about a wonderful dinner he had made for them, or they reminisced about his perfect martinis. One neighbor said that she had recently moved to the building and found herself living next to Edward. Shortly after she moved in, she broke her leg and Edward arrived on her doorstep with a plate of food. When she told him that her mother was there taking care of her, Edward excused himself and returned minutes later with another plate of food. "For your mother," he said.

What has touched you most about readers' reactions to the book?

I'm thrilled that readers seem genuinely interested in my friend Edward. What moves them most—and I've gathered this from the comments people make at readings I've done—is that Edward took so much time and made such an effort to lovingly prepare food for friends. Food really is love. Plus, readers have responded to the fact that Edward reveled in introducing one friend to another, in making those connections over a meal. In this day and age when we're all so busy, and when connecting through Facebook and other social media platforms sometimes replaces face-to-face encounters, Edward's example is a reminder that there's no substitute for sitting down in the real world with real friends and just talking, laughing, sharing. It's important. It's necessary. I often think of that day—and I mention this in this book—that I went over to Edward's apartment for dinner and he was making oysters Rockefeller. It was an elaborate process and I said, "What's the occasion, Edward?" His response was to shrug his shoulders and say, "Do we need one?"

What recipes of Edward's do you continue to make?

I still make everything! I love to do his soufflés, especially the apricot soufflé. I always roast chicken Edward's way—in a paper bag, with herbs and vegetables. I make apple galettes often, whenever I have old apples lying around. And because of Edward I'm not afraid to attempt anything, no matter how daunting it may look. It doesn't always work out perfectly but I'm brave and bold in the kitchen. And that's all due to Edward.

Could you share a recipe for one of Edward's dishes that you don't have in the book?

Rémoulades are these amazing mayonnaise sauces. Essentially, you take an egg yolk, beat it with lemon juice, salt, and olive oil to make your mayonnaise, and add a pinch of harissa, which is a North African paste made up of different kinds of chili peppers. When I get lazy, I squeeze in some of the harissa that I bought in a tube at a North African shop in the south of France last summer. Following Edward's lead, I sometimes slice fresh fennel bulbs on a mandoline and then cover them with the rémoulade. So easy and so delicious!

What are some of your favorite places to shop for food these days?

I will shop anywhere, but I love a good fish market, like one on Long Island called Mastic Seafood. It's near the Mastic-Shirley station. I buy sea urchins or oysters or *bacalhau* (salted cod) there because everything is so unbelievably fresh. It's also relatively inexpensive. I stay away from high-priced gourmet food shops. Good food doesn't have to cost a lot of money. Something else I learned from Edward.

Since Edward introduced you to cooking and baking have you continued to expand your repertoire? What interests you lately?

I've begun baking sourdough bread. You need to be dedicated because a loaf takes more than three days to prepare. And I use the sourdough *levain* (or starter) to make everything from pizza dough to waffles and even biscotti. There's something special about how *levain* shapes the taste and the texture of the dough. It's chewy, slightly sour (in a good way), and much more substantial than bread that is made just with white flour. I have also started grinding different kinds of rye and wheat berries. The other day, I made the most sublime pasta with a mixture of white and whole wheat freshly ground flours.

It must be hard to find time to cook. Is your job as a reporter still as crazy as it seems in the book? Do you and Melissa have new places to eat on stakeouts and stressful days?

In many ways, my job has become even more hectic. I discovered a place in Grand Central Station called Meyers Bageri, which is a Danish bakery/café. Melissa and I both go there often between assignments. These bakeries—there is also one in Brooklyn—were opened by the Danish chef Claus Meyer, who also has a well-known restaurant in Copenhagen. The bakery will even give you some *levain* if you bring your own container! I recently tried the rye bread, which is dense and studded with fresh rye berries. It blew me away.

Edward never seems to use a recipe. Do you? If so, what are some of your favorite cookbooks or food websites?

I do consult recipes, though I also improvise a lot. I have a terrific book from the King Arthur Flour Company that I use for baking. And I am always looking up classic recipes in Julia Child's books. I love, love, love anything that Yotam Ottolenghi does. He's an Israeli-born, London-based chef, and his recipes mostly center around vegetables. He has a great recipe for roasted eggplant topped with couscous flavored with roasted pine nuts and raisins. I also like to make his green beans with parsley-tahini paste that you whip up with fresh parsley, tahini, olive oil, and garlic. He has introduced me to preserved lemons and rose and orange blossom essences, and *za'atar*, which is a mixture of sumac, sesame seeds, and oregano. You can dip bread in *za'atar*-flavored olive oil, and it gives the bread a deep, earthy flavor. Can you tell I'm very into bread these days?

Writing the book was an emotional experience for you. How did you handle that?

Oh, it was the best therapy. It was actually the most pleasurable writing I have ever done! I was always happy to sit down and write, as I did at 4:00 a.m. every morning when I was working on the book. It was the most peaceful time in my day. Emotionally, the hardest thing was being brutally honest about my experiences. Edward was obviously very dear to me, but I didn't want to write about him in a way that was maudlin and oversentimentalized.

Is it harder to write about events in your personal life than it is to cover a story or do investigative journalism?

It was far harder to write about my personal life than to report a journalistic piece. Still, both require the element of truth—that brutal honesty I mentioned. I have always felt I have a contract with my reader. So whether as a reporter or as a memoirist, I owe readers the truth, or as close as I can get to it, anyway.

Since clearly authenticity matters to you, how did you remember all the specific moments in your relationship with Edward?

From the very first dinner I had with Edward, I felt the need, a compulsion almost, to go home and write everything down. It wasn't because I was planning to write a book at that time. It was all about making the moment last, savoring the dinner and the company and the jazz for as long as I could by recording it all. In my journal, I wrote down everything we ate, everything Edward said, because most of the time dinner with Edward was magical.

AN IMPRINT OF PUSHKIN PRESS

ONE – an imprint of Pushkin Press – is the home of our English language publishing from around the world. The list is as varied as it is distinct, encompassing new voices and established names, fiction and non-fiction. Our stories range from dystopian tales to comic ones, prizewinning novels to memoirs. We select only a small handful of titles each year, and publish them with particular care and attention, which means that every book is a gem. And what makes them ONE? Compelling writing, unique voices, great stories.

SHE WOULD BE KING
Wayétu Moore

NUMBER ONE CHINESE RESTAURANT
Lillian Li

ONLY KILLERS AND THIEVES
Paul Howarth

SYMPATHY
Olivia Sudjic

AMONG THE LIVING AND THE DEAD
Inara Verzemnieks

THE FISHERMEN
Chigozie Obioma

THE EXTRA MAN
Jonathan Ames

LAYOVER
Lisa Zeidner

THE BEAUTIFUL BUREAUCRAT
Helen Phillips

SCHOOL OF VELOCITY
Eric Beck Rubin